USING TECHNOLOGY
TO CREATE VALUE

Using Technology to Create Value

Designing the Tools for the New HR Function

Allan Boroughs and
Cat Rickard

GOWER

Published by
Gower Publishing Limited
Wey Court East
Union Road
Farnham
Surrey GU9 7PT
England

Gower Publishing Company
Suite 420
101 Cherry Street
Burlington, VT 05401-4405
USA

www.gowerpublishing.com

British Library Cataloguing in Publication Data
Boroughs, Allan.
  Using technology to create value : designing the tools for
  the new HR function. -- (The Gower HR transformation series)
  1. Personnel management--Technological innovations.
  2. Personnel management--Data processing.
  I. Title II. Series III. Rickard, Cat.
  658.3'00285-dc22

  ISBN: 978-0-566-08827-8 (pbk)
  ISBN: 978-0-7546-8162-5 (ebk)

Library of Congress Cataloging-in-Publication Data
Boroughs, Allan.
  Using technology to create value : designing the tools for the new HR
  function/by Allan Boroughs and Cat Rickard.
    p. cm. -- (The Gower HR transformation series)
  Includes bibliographical references and index.
  ISBN 978-0-566-08827-8 (pbk) 1. Personnel management--Technological
  innovations. 2. Management information systems. I. Rickard, Cat. II. Title.
  HF5549.5.T33B673 2009
  658.3001'1--dc22

                                                              2009016483

Mixed Sources
Product group from well-managed
forests and other controlled sources
www.fsc.org Cert no. SA-COC-1565
© 1996 Forest Stewardship Council

Printed and bound in Great Britain by
MPG Books Group, UK

Contents

List of Figures   *vii*
List of Tables   *ix*
Introduction   *xi*

1   HR Roles and Their Technology Needs   1
2   Defining What You Really Need   27
3   Making the Case for Technology   43
4   Selecting the Right Vendor   65
5   Designing and Implementing the Service   85
6   Top 10 Tips for Success   109

List of Figures

1.1	The 'New' HR model	2
1.2	Typical issues reducing the impact of technology on the HR function	6
1.3	Top technology for HR	8
1.4	SSC technology	14
1.5	CRM in detail	15
1.6	Screen shot of best practice knowledge management system	23
2.1	Impact of poor systems	29
2.2	HR strategy and implications for HR systems	35
2.3	Recruitment and resourcing process – Recruitment	38
4.1	HR systems market overview	67
4.2	HR RFP table of contents	74
4.3	Example vendor scoresheet	77
4.4	Summary vendor scoring	77
5.1	HRIS project phases	86

List of Tables

1.1	Key HR technologies	9–10
1.2	Different functionalities	12–13
1.3	Methods for contacting the SSCs	17
1.4	HRBP Management information requirements	20–21
3.1	Using software suppliers to support business case development	49
3.2	Cost components for the HRIS business case	51–52
3.3	Contents of a Project Initiation Document (PID)	57–60
4.1	Typical areas covered in a formal evaluation plan	75–76
4.2	Orion Partners top tips for vendor demonstrations	79–81
5.1	Key components of project management	88–89
5.2	Solution build activities	96–98
5.3	Types of testing	102
5.4	Rollout preparation activities	104
5.5	Closure checklist	106

Introduction

This book provides an insight into how technology can enable effective delivery of the HR service, together with an overview of how this technology can be selected and implemented into your organisation successfully. Beginning with an overview of the key roles within HR and how technology can support them, it provides a step-by-step guide detailing how to identify your requirements, develop a compelling business case, select a solution, ensure the design of the technology solution addresses HR and business priorities and implement the solution.

This book includes suggestions on the skills required to implement HR Technology (HRT) effectively, as well as some of the topics expanded on further in the companion book in this series, *Managing HR Transformation: Realising the New HR Function*. Case studies are included to illustrate the types of issues and decisions that need to be taken, as well as the solutions that have been developed within other organisations.

During the 1970s and 1980s, as organisations began to invest more significantly in IT solutions, IT providers began to develop generic solutions that could be sold to multiple organisations. These solutions focused initially on back office functions, in the first instance on finance (including financial control and asset management), and offered the potential to be significantly cheaper to implement than developing bespoke, custom built solutions for each organisation.

HR AND ERP

In the late 1980s and 1990s the first Enterprise Resource Planning (ERP) solutions appeared which combined the functionality of procurement, sales order processing, distribution, production management, engineering and plant maintenance on a single integrated IT platform. The basic premise was to provide an integrated solution, where data was captured only once and was capable of supporting the requirements of the entire organisation. It was not long before HR came within the scope of these solutions. Payroll and time and attendance management formed the initial targets for inclusion, closely linked as they are with the financial aspects of the organisation. Also staff administration increasingly became a focus area for integration.

EMERGENCE OF 'BEST OF BREED'

Over time, however, the technology landscape for HR became more complicated. Many of the ERP providers were slow to develop a full range of functionality in their HR solutions. As a result, a number of smaller providers developed specific solutions in parallel for areas such as learning administration, recruitment and resourcing, career and succession planning and compensation and performance management. These solutions were often developed with the aid of HR practitioners and provided a very close fit in terms of the functionality required by HR. Many organisations chose to adopt a 'best of breed' approach to their technology solutions, using a mainstream ERP provider for business processing, outsourcing their payroll solutions and using a mix and match of technologies to service HR.

The downside of this approach included increased maintenance costs to build and maintain the interfaces between different applications; a costly process that added risk to the project. Where solutions were not adequately integrated, it often resulted in duplication of data , increased costs of maintenance and increased likelihood of inaccurate information being captured. In such an environment, consistent reporting across multiple applications and geographies is always challenging.

NEW HR STRUCTURES

By the year 2000 the picture was further complicated by the introduction of the Shared Service Centre (SSC) concept, an organisational development that ensured economies of scale were captured through grouping transactional processing together (for example, finance, HR and IT). The introduction of automated employee administration, in particular manager and employee self-service applications, enabled administration to be centralised, resulting in significant savings in terms of HR headcount. By this point the work of David Ulrich and others had led to the development of the 'three legged stool' structure for HR, comprising three organisational elements; one focused on economies of scale and process efficiency via the SSC; one focused on business centred value added HR activities via the Business Partners; and finally with the Centre of Expertise (CoE) providing overall policy support and advice to the organisation.

WHERE ARE WE NOW?

There is a wide variation in the stages of development exhibited by different HR organisations. Some organisations' teams have already implemented the full Ulrich model across a consistent technology platform and are running mature shared service centre operations and business partner models; other organisations still have multiple systems in place and are at varying points along the transformation journey. The questions HR leaders ask tend, however, to be similar regardless of where they are on this continuum.

- What is the business case for using technology to support our service?

- How do we maximise our existing assets?

- Should we start all over and buy in a new integrated technology solution?

- How can we better support our Business Partners, CoE, SSCs and managers and staff using technology?

- How do we keep sight of our priorities when reviewing available solutions?

- How can we work more effectively with our IT teams?

This book explores the answers to these questions and provides an outline of some of the key decisions and issues that must be addressed if HR is to take control of technology and ensure it delivers what the business truly needs. We will start with a review of the technology demands of the emerging roles in the new HR model.

① HR Roles and Their Technology Needs

INTRODUCTION – HUMAN RESOURCES HAS CHANGED

The development of the Human Resources (HR) function is bound inextricably to the technologies that support it and the pace of change in HR has often been dictated by the ability of technology solutions to service the function effectively. Recent improvements in the speed of technology implementation and the capabilities of IT solutions have now presented HR with new opportunities to improve the way in which it delivers services to the business.

Delivery of an effective HR service is typically dependent on the capabilities of the organisation structure, development of a streamlined end-to-end process and the integration of effective technology. However, the organisation structures typically found within HR functions today are increasingly different to those in place when the majority of technology solutions were first designed and the ability to use HR technology effectively is dependent on a clear understanding of how the new model for HR works and the demands of the various roles within it.

AN EVOLVED HR

It is important to remember that while technology is a key enabler in the modern HR function, technology cannot take the credit for the evolution of HR from the role of traditional record keeper and personnel administrator to that of a strategic business partner. Much of the impetus for this change is credited to the work of David Ulrich and others.

Ulrich's model emphasised the need for HR to be a *strategic* partner to the business and to become much more business and customer-focused, cost efficient, innovative and structured in such a way that it could respond quickly to changing priorities. Ulrich proposed that HR should focus efforts in three key areas of activity; the Strategic Business Partner; the administrative expert within a Shared Services Environment and the HR expert within the Centre of Expertise (See Figure 1.1). Collectively these roles enable HR to deliver high value, efficient and effective people services to the organisation when adequately supported by the right technology tools.

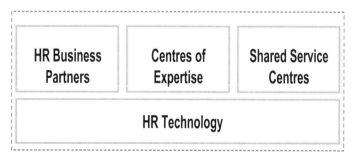

Figure 1.1   The 'New' HR model

If technology is to support HR in delivering an effective service to the business, it must cater to the specific requirements of these three roles. It is critical first to examine how these roles operate in practice and the requirements each has for HR information.

ROLES WITHIN THE EVOLVED HR TEAM

The HR Business Partner (HRBP) role represents a shift away from the generalist HR manager, towards a role that is more closely aligned with the business objectives. The role frequently involves physically locating within business units to maintain a close understanding of the business's needs and objectives.

While there is still the need to deploy a broad range of technical HR knowledge as a Business Partner, the main responsibility is to add value through delivering people interventions that are directly geared to support the achievement of business objectives. The ability to influence strategy, as opposed to merely executing against it, is fundamental to this process.

To operate effectively, Business Partners need:

- The credibility to engage with the business.

- To be integrated into the management team to enable them to understand the strategic objectives of the business and to influence key people related decisions.

- The ability to challenge effectively, and to 'think outside the box'.

3

- Deep influencing, change and transition management skills.

- Access to the right support, both technical and administrative, to enable them to deliver.

Shared Service Centres (SSC) typically manage all transactional activities between employees and HR through a coordinated set of channels. Although the scope of the SSC will depend on the nature of the organisation (that is, size, complexity, location, market), the key to SSC success is the development of administrative excellence through standardisation and centralisation and the ability to leverage economies of scale by handling large transactional volumes.

The Shared Service Centre is pivotal in ensuring other parts of HR are able to focus on value- added activities, by dealing with all administrative transactions and filtering enquiries rapidly to the appropriately skilled resource.

The Centre of Expertise (CoE) comprises team members with specialist skills that are not widely distributed across the organisation and which may be centralised to drive economies of scale.

Activities covered by the CoE will vary according to the nature of the challenges faced by the business, its size, complexity and geography. For example, in Retail Banking those responsible for handling serious disciplinary and grievance cases will typically reside in the CoE. In a manufacturing environment, employee relations specialists will travel to local sites to provide hands-on advice and support to managers. Activities are included in the scope of the CoE if they require deep process and technical knowledge.

The Centre of Expertise is predominantly about providing specialist technical and professional support as distinct from the high volume, service orientated transactional capabilities of the SSC. The adoption of a CoE generates a number of benefits:

- Experience in specialist areas (pay and benefits, pensions, performance management, employee relations, and so on) easily accessible by the whole organisation.

- Learning shared across the experts.

- Greater consistency in interpreting policy for the business.

- Expert staff more efficiently deployed.

HOW DOES TECHNOLOGY ALLOW HR TO ACHIEVE ITS MANDATE?

It is both the strength and the weakness of HR systems that they carry a high degree of functionality, are generally available to all and are easy to acquire. It is easy therefore to create an illusion of progress by going out and buying software without truly understanding how the application will be used by the business.

To make an intelligent start on the assessment of technology needs, a review of current technology failings can provide insight into the issues that constrain the HR function in different ways (see Figure 1.2).

Operational Issues *'It stops us working'*	Tactical Issues *'It stops us managing'*	Strategic Issues *'It stops us changing'*
➢Data is not complete ➢Data is inaccurate ➢We lack basic information ➢We are drowning in paper ➢Data sits in several places ➢System requires a lot of manual intervention ➢People aren't getting paid accurately and on time	➢The system does not cover everyone ➢Only a few people can access data ➢We lack qualitative data in critical areas – e.g. skills ➢We have no reporting tools ➢Data on different systems does not agree	➢There is no end-to-end process ➢System drives the process not the other way around ➢No flexibility to change process ➢System will not support a new organizational model for HR ➢No universal access to PCs – dated IT architecture ➢We cannot forecast trends – we only know what happened in the past

Figure 1.2   Typical issues reducing the impact of technology on the HR function

For the Shared Service Centre, the key considerations will converge on supporting the revised end to end process in the operations centre. This will be coupled with a need to drive new types of management information to monitor service performance and financial re-charging.

For the HR Business Partner, key considerations at this stage will be how these types of issues impact clients within the business and how the HR solution will have the potential to help them. The lack of critical qualitative data is likely to be a key issue for senior managers and a key consideration for the Business Partner when defining their toolset requirements.

Access to 'key people indicators' relating to pay, benefits and performance are likely to be high on the shopping list for the Business Partner's clients. But good management information will be irrelevant if HR cannot underpin this with robust core processes relating to pay, resourcing and development, particularly if they are an essential element of senior management strategy. Failure to deliver in these areas, either now or in the future, is always going to be a major barrier to the overall credibility of HR.

The Centres of Expertise, as the primary guardian of policy and policy interpretation, need to be able to communicate policy effectively to team members, other HR staff and the organisation as a whole. The ability to share new information quickly and easily is critical if timely updates to policy are to be implemented.

Figure 1.3 illustrates how the defined roles in the HR organisation create a mix of needs ranging from transactional requirements that focus on streamlining processes and automating operations to demands for sophisticated workforce analytics to extrapolate organisational trends and plan future policy and strategy.

While technology can offer huge benefits, the use of modern HR technologies frequently represents a radical departure from historic ways of working and can create resistance if not properly understood by the organisation or if not deployed appropriately. For example, employee and manager self service provides the means to devolve HR tasks to employees and line managers and allow data to be input only once, at source.

Self service examples include: allowing staff to book their own leave or nominate themselves for training; providing managers with the tools to approve staff requests, review information about their teams and manage processes relating to recruitment and performance management more effectively. Such tools are an important contributor to delivering efficiency savings in the HR SSC by releasing HR resources from low-value

7

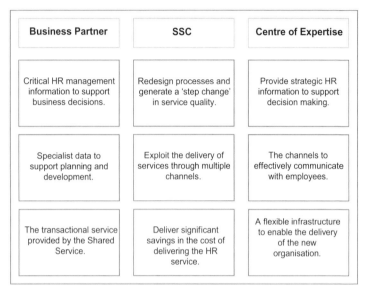

Figure 1.3   Top technology for HR

transactional activity while providing managers with greater information and control over their own staff.

As beneficial as these tools may appear, however, they will receive little favour in an organisation where everyone is not fully office based. Organisations in manufacturing, construction, healthcare, logistics and retail employ large numbers of managers and staff who have little or no access to desktop computers to manage such transactions.

Staff working in this situation often need to carry out self service transactions outside the scope of their daily work, sometimes even having to log on after hours from home. It is not surprising that, under these circumstances, managers and staff see little benefit in the new ways of working seeing them as having made their roles more difficult.

Against this background, we have set out below (Table 1.1) some guidance as to the types of technology on offer and their appropriateness in different situations. These are described more fully later in this section.

Table 1.1 Key HR technologies

Key technology solutions to support the new HR model		
Role	**Technologies**	**Considerations**
Employees and Line managers	Self service tools provide access to staff information, allow management of transactional processes and disseminate management information.	• Staff access to infrastructure may not be universal across the organisation. • Changes to working practices must be properly assessed and communicated to staff who are affected – benefits will not be felt if staff do not accept the new processes or technologies.
Shared Service Centre	Customer contact technologies and Customer relationship management (CRM) systems – track and manage queries and contacts and ensure continuity to the call centre process.	• CRM tools should be appropriate to the volume of activity that the contact centre experiences. • In situations where call volumes are high, integration with underlying HR data to identify callers and access records is essential.
	Workflow automation ensures correct routing of HR transactions, applies administrative rules and directs reminders and notifications to the right people in the organisation.	• Workflow automation relies on aspects of organisation management to ensure that information is routed to the tight person in the organisation. The extent to which processes can be successfully automated will rely on the quality of organisation data.

Table 1.1   *Concluded*

Key technology solutions to support the new HR model		
Role	**Technologies**	**Considerations**
Business Partners	Different levels of Management Information (MI): • Ad-hoc reporting and information. • Complex reports to monitor people related performance factors. • Workforce analytics to prepare trend analyses and forecasts.	• Dependent on data quality and the effectiveness of operational processes.
Centres of Excellence	Information portals to provide general access to key policy data and information. Knowledge management tools allowing staff to readily access information and answer queries. 'Best of breed' solutions to tackle specialist tasks in the organisation (for example, compensation planning).	• Adopt mix of approaches to knowledge management – a combination of frequently asked questions; on line policy guides and intelligent key word searches will maximise users' ability to find information they are looking for. • Best of breed applications should be fully integrated with underlying HR technologies and should avoid the need to maintain HR data in separate locations.

The following sections provide a more detailed insight into the types of technology that can be used to support each element of the new HR model. The demand for these applications amongst the business and HR communities and the impact that such solutions can have must be fully understood before embarking on a programme of costly development.

1) SHARED SERVICE CENTRE TECHNOLOGIES – OVERVIEW

While administrative efficiencies are not wholly dependent on technology, the scale of operations created by centralising operations across a large organisation demands some level of automation. For example, a large financial institution may routinely handle:

- 10,000 recruits a year from around 100,000 applicants.

- 6,000 leavers.

- 3,000 staff on maternity leave.

- 25,000 calls a month.

To manage this volume of activity successfully at low cost and high performance levels clearly demands the intervention of technology on several levels.

At its heart, the SSC embraces all of the administrative activities behind the core HR service lines (recruitment, performance management, training, employee relations, pay and benefits, pensions and leavers, information systems and vendor management), and therefore requires an effective intrinsic HR system to carry out core processing and maintain staff records in an integrated and efficient manner. Table 1.2 summarises some of the functions of these applications.

Beyond the traditional HR processing roles Shared Service Centres embrace a new service ethos requiring staff to be treated with exactly the same care and attention as external customers. As a result, the emergent HR SSC may itself now be divided into a transaction-oriented back-office together with a customer-facing front office. This in turn creates a new set of demands for technologies such as Customer Relationship Management (CRM) systems to support the interaction between the SSC and its customers.

Table 1.2   Different functionalities

New technology tools	Their use
Recruitment Management Systems (RMS)	• Create vacancies. • Advertise internally (intranet) and externally (via the web and 3rd party sites). • Administer multiple vacancy applications. • Manage the selection process using workflow routes between applicant/HR/line. • Manage administration (that is, contracts/references). • Generate MI (that is, available positions, interview schedules).
Learning Management Systems (LMS)	• Used by managers, employees and training staff to plan and administer all types of learning intervention, for example, courses, e-learning and coaching. • Holds data around a catalogue of learning options, pre-requisites, course dates, competency/learning requirements associated with positions/jobs and employee learning data (learning plan, training history, competencies, qualifications and so on). • May also serve as a platform from which users can access e- learning.

Table 1.2   *Concluded*

New technology tools	Their use
Talent management and succession planning software	• Record who is identified as having the potential for different senior roles in the organisations and what development they will require. • Can displays results graphically to provide a highly visual view of the succession plan, highlighting where key gaps may exist.
Benefits administration	• Makes payroll deductions and generate lists of scheme participants. • Provides data on membership details and scheme rules may either reside on the HRIS's benefits module or on a separate system. • May be used to administer flexible benefits schemes whereby salary is sacrificed to purchase a range of employee related products and services, for example, additional holiday or a private health insurance plan.

As we have seen, the move to shared services also demands flexibility in the way services are delivered to the business with not all users being able to access self service tools. This has given rise to a range of 'channel technologies' which govern the access that users have to the services of the SSC.

Finally, alongside each layer of technology is the requirement for Management Information (MI) to support the needs of a wide range of audiences. Figure 1.4 provides an indication of how these technologies work in an integrated environment.

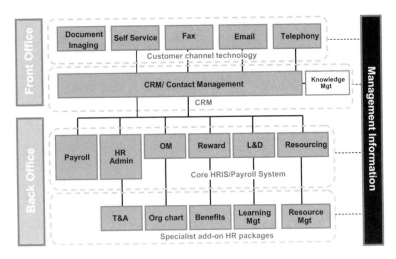

Figure 1.4   SSC technology

CUSTOMER RELATIONSHIP MANAGEMENT (CRM) TECHNOLOGIES

The CRM solution drives a number of management processes around the allocation and recording of work passing through the service centre (See Figure 1.5).

Specific tasks include:

- *Recording contacts:* record details of all contacts, maintaining a comprehensive contact history to be available to the agent when dealing with an employee. It also creates useful management information, for example, which types of query or which channels are generating the most usage.

- *Answering queries:* As the HR SSC aims to answer and close most calls on the spot, the CRM can enable this by providing a range of information including:

  - Contact history of all of the caller's previous contact as background data.
  - Direct access to employee personal records to provide critical information on the employee's terms and conditions and personal history.
  - Scripts to prompt the agent to complete basic activities such as security checks before answering the query.
  - Details of HR policies, processes, procedures and terms and conditions captured within an electronic knowledge base.

CRM – Main functions

Within shared services the CRM in the HR SSC has a number of important functions, specifically it will:

- Provide a record of all customer contacts.
- Help a SSC agent to clarify and answer a customer's query.
- Automate and streamline the allocation and processing of cases that is, work that results from a customer contact.
- Control the throughput of work within the shared service centre.
- Provide management information to assist resource planning and management, and monitoring of the SSC's performance against its service level agreements.
- Deliver full shared services automation by integrating the contact channels (self-service, phone, paper and so on) to the back-office data processing applications such as HRIS/payroll.

Figure 1.5   CRM in detail

- *Allocating and processing work:* Many enquiries require further action before they can be closed, for example, a request by a line manager for the HR SSC to carry out a transaction (also known as service requests or cases).

- *Managing work:* With all HR SSC work tracked through the CRM, the system provides a continual snapshot of completed, outstanding or pending work. In a fully automated HR SSC, every contact and transaction is logged on the system so all work can be monitored and managed; a radically different approach to the operation of the traditional HR office.

- *Management Information (MI):* The work management facilities described above are the most operational of several layers of management information available from the CRM system. Such operational data would typically be used to make hourly or daily management decisions, for example, work-reallocation, resource redeployment and so on. As with telephony, appropriate data can be displayed on wallboards to provide a visible snapshot of key performance indicators (KPIs), such as the number of cases outstanding.

CUSTOMER CONTACT METHODS – CUSTOMER CHANNEL TECHNOLOGIES

As discussed, the shared services model will frequently allow customers to access the service through a variety of communication channels – paper, email, fax, telephony and so on (see Table 1.3). These channels, described below, can now be integrated with other elements of the HR technology infrastructure, particularly the CRM solution, to deliver process efficiencies.

Table 1.3   Methods for contacting the SSCs

Tools	Purpose	CRM interface
Document imaging and fax technologies	Allows HR SSC to reduce paper coming into the office.	Documents are scanned into image format and stored and indexed within an Electronic Document and Records Managements system (eDRMS), which are passed automatically by the eDRMS to the CRM automatically opening a contact record.
Email	An alternative route for the employee to raise a query with the SSC. Note: Many service centres do not allow contact by email because the content is too unstructured. One compromise is more structured electronic forms ('eforms').	Creates a new contact record for action by an HR agent when the email reaches the CRM's email inbox. The customer will include the contact reference number on any subsequent email, so the new contact can easily be added to or associated with the previous one.
Telephony	Can record and store calls for training purposes or to retain a record of important conversations. Tools used: • Call transfer. • Routing calls to first available agent. • Callers stating basic information.	Creates accessible MI. Enables performance to be measured against HR SSC service standards including: • Calls taken. • Calls waiting and lost. • Average pick-up times.

SELF SERVICE TOOLS

Self-service is increasingly important in the delivery of the new HR service model. The ability to devolve HR tasks to employees and the line, thereby streamline the work by automation, is a key contributor to delivering efficiency savings in the HR SSC. For example, the input work previously undertaken by HR administrators upon receipt of forms completed by staff or the line manager is no longer necessary. For their part, the line manager or employee are merely entering on screen the same data that they had previously been completing manually. Providing the change management issues are adequately addressed in the implementation process, the change should be seen as a positive advantage.

Self-service falls into two categories – view-only and update. With view-only access, a member of staff might use employee self-service (ESS) to view their payslip or a list of training courses, while a manager might use manager self-service to examine an absence report or an HR policy on-line. Update access would be used to allow an employee to request overtime and a manager to approve it.

Self service tools are generally coupled with the use of workflow technologies; in simple terms these refer to tools that allow the rules of an administrative process to be automated and which will route an administrative task to the appropriate person or role in the organisation. Thus employees may use self service to nominate themselves for training which triggers a workflow activity to inform their manager and seek their approval.

2) BUSINESS PARTNERS – MANAGEMENT INFORMATION (MI)

The primary goal of the HR Business Partner is to develop close relationships with the businesses they serve and demonstrate their capability to make a commercial impact in the execution of people strategies. This requires hard factual knowledge from management information, which may be categorised in several ways:

- Operational MI to support ongoing processes – for example, calls lost, cases awaiting attention, or interview schedules (HRIS or RMS).

- Tactical MI to determine and measure HR performance and the effectiveness of HR policies, for example, identifying the take-up of a recently-introduced benefits, comparing absence statistics across departments, or analysing learning plans to identify where corporate learning initiatives might be needed.

- Strategic information used to supply senior management with a view of a defined set of business-critical indicators.

- Although the SSC management teams are likely to be the major users of operational management information, the tactical MI and virtually all strategic MI is used outside of the HR SSC by the HRBPs, line managers and corporate executives.

To pull together the full range of management information required in the role, the HRBP will need the HRIS to demonstrate a number of characteristics as illustrated in Table 1.4.

Table 1.4   HRBP Management information requirements

HRBP MI requirement	MI tools
Rapid response to management requests or queries	• Ad-hoc reporting tools – simple enquiry language coupled with the ability to produce simple on screen reports and make these available to others via email or accessible via a web browser. • Query tools should incorporate the ability to deliver both statistics, for example, numbers of staff qualifying for a certain benefit, analysed by grade, and lists, for example, of the staff concerned sorted alphabetically within department.
Routine monitoring of key performance indicators and service levels	• Regular standard reports covering key topics such as headcount analysis, absence information and status of recruitment campaigns. • Standard reporting tools allow for complex analyses and manipulation of data to be produced quickly and routinely as part of regular reporting cycles. • The high degree of flexibility offered by these tools allow for a wide range of queries and formats to be produced but can take some time to configure.
Modelling tools	• Some aspects of the HRBPs role may require modeling of different scenarios (for example, potential outcomes of a sucession planning exercise) or manipulation of figures (for example, allocating an available bonus pool on the basis of performance). • Such operations may require data to be exported from the HR system (for example, salary and performance data) to be manipulated externally. • Whilst spreadsheets have historically been used extensively for this purpose they have limited capabilities to control the data effectively and it can be difficult to 'reload' data into the system once the modeling is complete. • Modern modeling tools offer an integrated solution for extracting data, manipulating it and loading it back into the core system. Whilst stand alone solutions are available, these are increasingly a feature of a core HR application.

Table 1.4   *Concluded*

HRBP MI requirement	MI tools
Workforce analytics – the ability to combine people related data from multiple sources, spot trends in data and predict outcomes	• Organisations increasingly demand a cross functional perspective, for example, combining financial data, staff performance, salary data and scheduling information to produce accurate project resource plans. • Workforce analytics tools offer the potential to combine multiple sources of data and present it in sophisticated graphical formats to allow the business partner to spot historical and future trends. • Such analytics tools may be used to build dashboards or balanced scorecards that can provide real-time indications of issues and problem areas.
Complex graphical outputs – for example, organisation charting tools and workforce planning tools	• This may require specialist add on solutions but will need to integrate with core HRIS data so that organograms and so on, may be produced directly from the data in the core HR solution.
Data archiving	• The need to produce management information that monitors trends over extended periods (for example, comparison of absence rates over several years) may require facilities to archive data in a way that allows analyses to be carried out without compromising the performance of the system, for example, by avoiding the need to store large amounts of historical data on line.

3) CENTRES OF EXPERTISE (COE) – KNOWLEDGE MANAGEMENT

The Centre of Excellence role is predominantly about providing specialist technical and professional support to the business and other areas of HR on specialist HR topics. Professionals within CoE roles may therefore possess many of the same requirements as the HRBPs for ready access to a wide range of management information to support decision making and planning.

However, there are also unique needs in this area which may require access to a specialist range of tools. For example the development of policies and distribution of policy data may benefit from the use of knowledge management tools which provide a mechanism for disseminating accurate, up to date and consistent information on policies and processes to employees and managers. Effective, knowledge management systems may include the following characteristics:

- Provide access for all managers and employees within the organisation by means of a company portal which is simple to understand, user friendly and easy to access.

- Provide a wide range of information and data on topics of relevance to managers and staff.

- Be widely communicated to employees so that they know how to access information and develop an ethos of 'consulting the portal first' before calling HR.

- Be regularly updated so that users have confidence in the information they receive.

- Allow for data to be accessed at several different levels. For example, the availability of full policy documentation; key word searches; frequently asked questions and user guidance notes.

- Provide data in a clearly laid out format which is simple to navigate.

- Perform well in terms of access time for queries and time taken to load new information.

An example page from a 'best practice' knowledge management system is shown in Figure 1.6.

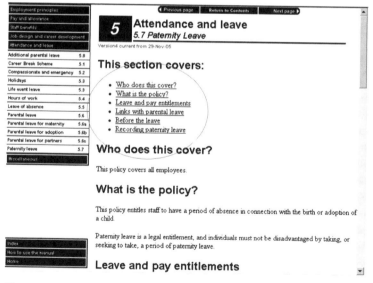

Figure 1.6 **Screen shot of best practice knowledge management system**

In combination with the use of knowledge management tools, CoE teams may require access to a range of other solutions to support their specialist roles. Examples of these include:

- Web based resourcing/recruitment systems.

- Learning management system.

- Talent management and succession management tools.

- Benefits administration.

Though these applications may be wholly owned and managed by the SSCs, the specialists in the CoE will require access to the data they hold to inform policy decisions and need an awareness of the types of functions they carry out.

THINGS TO REMEMBER

- Developments in the way HR services are delivered have led to the creation of new roles in HR, each with their own unique demands of HR technology:

  - HR Business Partners.
  - HR Shared Services.
  - Centres of Expertise.

- The key to success in delivering HRIT is in understanding the demands of the business and the implications for HR in terms of transactional systems and the production of management information.

- Technology must be appropriate to the organisational context; what works in one industry should not be applied to all.

- To support the needs of different users in the organisation will require the effective integration of a broad set of applications including core HR and payroll applications, customer relationship management systems, self service and workflow, telephony and knowledge management systems.

- Although the focus of HR is to deliver one consistent service to the business, this can be enabled by a variety of different tools and technologies.

- The right tools will vary according to the area of HR to be enabled: SSC, BP or CoE.

- The IT market is constantly changing and developing new solutions – it is important to liaise closely with your IT colleagues to ensure you remain up to speed on what's out there.

- If you do have IT issues, make sure you prioritise them, and address them in the right order – this should be driven from the service you need to deliver to the business.

② Defining What You Really Need

'WHAT FIRE ARE YOU TRYING TO PUT OUT?'

Defining your requirements accurately and to an appropriate level of detail is essential if a robust business case is to be constructed. Furthermore, vendors must be briefed appropriately as part of the selection process. However, knowing what you need is more complicated than it sounds.

All too often, an HR team will approach this the wrong way, possibly as a result of attempting to follow an IT driven methodology. In many cases, the starting point is an exhaustive assessment of current processes often complicated by the fact that processes are not common across the organisation. The wider the geographic spread of the organisation or the larger the number of business units, the more likely this is to be the case. The level of information captured becomes highly detailed and the teams involved may become too focused on the specific steps within the processes themselves.

This results in a requirement that does not clearly specify the objective and outcome of the activity. It is no wonder that, at

27

best, this exercise produces information that is too detailed and too organisation specific to be of use in selecting a package solution. At worst, many organisations never move beyond the current process mapping stage. Where a new structure for HR delivery is to be introduced at the same time, the value of completing detailed process maps for the existing processes is also questionable due to the scale of the change that will be undertaken.

In other cases the HR team may engage early on with software providers and become distracted by the products on offer; failing to connect the exciting options available with what are often a far more prosaic set of basic requirements. In such cases, the solution put in place may be underutilised, and may even fail to meet the original requirements completely.

In our experience, it is essential that time is taken to define accurately both the required HR service and the technology solution that will enable this service.

'WHERE DOES IT HURT?' – CONDUCTING A CURRENT STATE ASSESSMENT

A useful first step in identifying future needs is to understand explicitly what is wrong with current systems. This involves carrying out a current state assessment as a basis for achieving a consensus amongst the main stakeholders as to what problem HR systems are intended to fix.

Organisations will start from different perspectives. Many will have an incumbent HRIS, possibly based on dated technology, that cannot deliver the type of information and process automation that the organisation now needs. Others may have undergone organisational changes, for example, implementing shared services that demand a higher level of sophistication from HR systems if the full benefits of the change are to be realised. One consideration is that there may be more than one legacy system in use in different parts of the organisation; the current state assessment will play a key part in determining which systems will be in line for replacement by the new system.

A good place to start is to focus on where the current 'pain points' are in the organisation and to examine what it is that current systems are stopping the organisation from doing. Such problems typically exist at several levels as illustrated in Figure 2.1.

Operational Issues *'It stops us working'*	Tactical Issues *'It stops us managing'*	Strategic Issues *'It stops us changing'*
➤Data is not complete ➤Data is inaccurate ➤We lack basic information ➤We are drowning in paper ➤Data sits in several places ➤System requires a lot of manual intervention ➤People aren't getting paid accurately and on time	➤The system does not cover everyone ➤Only a few people can access data ➤We lack qualitative data in critical areas – for example, skills ➤We have no reporting tools ➤Data on different systems does not agree	➤There is no end-to-end process ➤System drives the process not the other way around ➤No flexibility to change process ➤System will not support a new organisational model for HR ➤No universal access to PCs – dated IT architecture ➤We cannot forecast trends – we only know what happened in the past

Figure 2.1   Impact of poor systems

Much of this data may be gathered by talking to existing users at different levels in the organisation. Some data may already be available to inform the process, for example, performance against service level agreements, feedback from businesses, staff surveys, and so on.

Once the initial analysis has highlighted the issues that stakeholders at all levels in the organisation are having, it may be useful to review how the organisation is performing against commercially available benchmarks. These will typically enable the organisation to assess the performance of the HR function, processes and technology against industry standards.

Benchmarking data is often highly sophisticated and can provide comparative metrics based on size and sector. It is important to ensure you use relevant data for your organisation. Many organisations use management consultants at this stage to gain an external perspective on HR operational performance and also to advise how these issues might be addressed though HR technology. Such consultancies should have a good understanding of the HR systems market and be able to provide a list and provisional assessment of the main technology packages, their suppliers and potential implementation partners.

At the end of this process you should have a good picture of where the major problems reside, from an internal and external perspective and this information can now be used to help define the solution.

GETTING STARTED – WHOSE REQUIREMENT IS IT ANYWAY?

Recent research conducted by *Personnel Today* (Wilcock, 2006) identified that 60 per cent of HR professionals believed their function to be effective, while only 20 per cent of their senior colleagues in other functions agreed. Clearly HR is fundamentally failing to demonstrate it can deliver a service that is valued by its customers and organisation.

From the current state analysis, the HR team should now have an accurate view of how the existing system and service is perceived by customers and how it should be perceived in the future. Whatever HR delivers, it must be in line with the service required by the business and there must be clear expectations set regarding exactly what the service will and will not provide going forward. Failure to do this will result in a solution that will not be valued by the business and will enhance the perception that HR is ineffective.

This inevitably means starting the design process at the top of the organisation and agreeing with key business stakeholders what features of the HR service will really make a difference as to how their business is supported. Early investigation and analysis of these top level requirements with the senior team in the organisation will form the core design principles. This principles provide the anchor for how the whole solution will be designed, developed and implemented within the organisation.

Canvassing the key business stakeholders regarding what they value in existing HR services will provide an initial set of priorities for the design work. It also provides critical input for both the business case and the case for change, which can be used to ensure that IT providers understand the business objectives of the project and what it aims to achieve.

A well articulated set of design principles will form the touchstone for the service design to which the programme team can return when design decisions need to be taken. If the design principles are clear from the outset organisations will avoid one of the most common causes of failure, a gap between the objectives of the business and the tactical delivery plans put in place by HR.

Design principles should be articulated in terms of what the principle is, what this will mean for the business and what they will get as a result. Using examples with stakeholders when discussing and agreeing the principles will bring them to life and ensure they are practical guides rather than just theoretical statements.

For example, a principle which is to 'strike the right balance', that is, a fit for purpose solution rather than a gold plated one, should be backed up with examples relating to what this means in terms of service delivery. In this instance it could mean that although managers would like to have shared services cover 24/7, in practice they could work with a service that operates over standard business hours.

These principles will subsequently be used to inform the design of the structures, processes and technologies needed to deliver the required service.

WHAT IS OUR SCOPE?

Based on the service requirements of the organisation, together with a realistic appraisal of what investment the business will be prepared to make in the transformation programme, the programme team should begin to form a view of the model needed to deliver the new HR service. At this stage it will be important to have a view of the key activities that have most importance to the business and how costly these activities are. Again, drawing on the information obtained in the current state assessment, you should be in a position to answer basic questions such as:

- How effective are your basic processes? For example, what percentage of staff are paid incorrectly each month?

- How many people have we got in HR?

- What are some of the basic staff to HR ratios in place?

- What percentage of HR headcount is focused on value adding activities, as opposed to admin?

- Are staff using the existing systems in a timely and accurate manner?

- How many HR systems (including unofficial data repositories like spreadsheets) are in use currently?

- What is the current technology landscape?

- What is the cost of HR data entry? And HR data re-entry?

This information will form the basis of a list of priorities for areas that need to be addressed. Based on this information, work can begin on the operating model and service designs.

This should outline each stage of the employee lifecycle – for example, starting work, at work, building capability, performance and reward, leaving work – and highlight what the main activities are. Rather than mapping these as a process, it is often more productive to build these documents as service designs that define who (from each area of the operating model) does what to deliver the required outcome and service to the business. This approach will ensure the focus is kept on service delivery which will inform all areas of solution design, including structure, process and technology.

In our experience, developing service designs ensures that communication channels between the business and HR are accurately defined from the outset. Once the service has been nailed down, process maps can then be developed as part of the design phase of the programme to inform the development of IT requirements and an input to training design.

WHAT PRIORITY IS NEEDED?

Although the plan for implementation would typically be completed at a later stage, the business case will demand an early understanding of which elements of the service requirement carry greater priority. This prioritisation will depend entirely on the context of the organisation. A typical example might be:

1. Deliver effective time and attendance capture to address current inaccuracies in salary payments.

2. Centralise administration to reduce percentage of HR effort spent on basic administration.

3. Address recruitment issues.

4. Deliver more cost effective payroll services.

Each of these priorities will have implications for the work needed to deliver the overall service in terms of structure, process and technology. Figure 2.2 provides an example of how the components of business and HR strategy may combine to drive technology requirements.

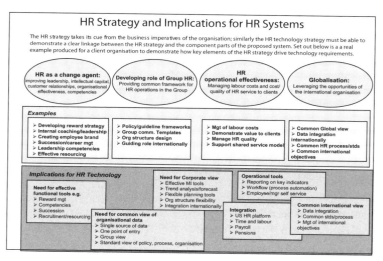

Figure 2.2   HR strategy and implications for HR systems

Any solution that does not address the need for robust core processes or closely integrated people systems is unlikely to produce meaningful management data. Unfortunately many organisations invest heavily in HR technology solutions without understanding this relationship and then, in spite of their investment, are unable to produce meaningful management information.

WHAT IS THE TECHNOLOGY REQUIREMENT?

Based on the operating model and the service designs, work should now be completed to put together the technology requirements. The understanding gained from developing these requirements will support the development of an IT budget for inclusion in the business case.

In developing these requirements it is essential to engage fully with your counterparts within the internal IT team. The delivery of HR technology to support the new service model in HR will require a marriage of skills encompassing a broad array of HR, IT and programme management capabilities. During the process of implementation and after the solution has been delivered, HR will have a critical dependence on the IT service to ensure the system is properly configured, managed and maintained. To achieve this level of support, IT will need to define its own requirements of the system relating to areas such as data integrity, security, system integration and networking. The early input of IT into the definition of requirements and selection of solutions is, therefore, absolutely critical.

Your IT team should be best placed to review any current IT solutions in place and determine whether they might be adapted to support the future requirements of the HR team, or whether a more widespread change is required. For example, if your initial changes only involve implementing a basic contact service for managers, it may be possible to use a case management module from your existing IT package rather than having to invest in an entirely new contact management system up front.

They should also be able to advise you on the format and level of detail needed to complete an initial set of IT requirements. Typically, these will take the form of a list of outcome driven statements prioritised into essential and desirable (or high, medium and low) requirements. An example extract from a typical requirements document is set out in Figure 2.3.

As discussed in the previous chapter, in defining your high level technology requirements it is important to include all aspects of technology needed, not just the core solution. For example, this could include the requirements for CRM technologies to support contact management in the SSC, the telephony system needed to manage customer calls or document scanning tools to capture paperwork.

KEEPING YOUR EYE ON THE MANAGEMENT INFORMATION

One of the hardest areas to define is the requirement for management information, not least because, until the details of the new service are understood, it is difficult for HR to envisage the types of management information they will want to measure. Typically it is also an area that is neglected from a technology perspective on the grounds that if the data is there it can be reported on.

Recruitment of 1,000 staff during 2007/2008 is a mission critical activity and there will be a heavy reliance on recruitment administration systems to support this process.

Recruitment systems will be expected to support web enabled e-recruitment processes, workflow and automated selection as well as ensuring complete integration of the recruitment process (for example, by ensuring using of a common unique reference number for all recruitment candidates and employees).

Ref	Description	Fit	H, M, L	Module Name
1	Access to on-line record of defined job specs by HR and managers.		H	
2	Vacancy details to be created by HR or managers.		H	
3	Ability to mandate certain requirements; for example, cost centre.		H	
4	On-line approval of vacancy by senior managers.		M	
5	Approved vacancies automatically placed on Corporate web site for access by employees, external applicants and agencies.		H	
6	Employees, external applicants, agencies and speculative applicants to be able to apply for vacancies, record their details and attach electronic CV's via the website.		H	
7	Ability for HR to scan applications and CV's and record applicant's details on the system.		H	
8	Provision of a CV database that can be searched by various criteria including skills.		H	

Figure 2.3   Recruitment and resourcing process – Recruitment

However, data mining and reporting can be complicated and it is important that discussions start early to define what the requirements will look like. This will avoid the situation where, later down the line, reports are sacrificed in order to ensure the core technology solution is completed. A full description of MI tools is provided in the previous chapter but, broadly, support production of three types of information:

- *Operational Management Information*: Refers to the day-to-day requirements for information to support ongoing operational processes. Key criteria for this type of MI include query tools that are simple to use, rapid access to appropriate systems and data (*I need it now!*) and the flexibility to respond to unpredictable questions.

- *Tactical Management Information*: If operational MI relates to day-to-day operations, tactical MI is about monitoring and analysing the progress and performance of HR operations. Examples include measurement of key performance indicators in HR, routine workforce statistics or standard payroll outputs. While this information may not be required instantly, it is likely to be needed consistently. The flexibility to extract data with different analyses, format outputs and schedule outputs to be produced automatically, is likely to be key.

- *Strategic Management Information*: Many organisations claim the need for strategic data as the primary driver for investment in new systems, although interestingly there appears to be no common view of what constitutes strategic MI in the HR function. If the organisation is starting from a baseline of having no MI then the ability to produce some fairly basic statistics can feel quite strategic. Software suppliers have responded with a range of tools that fall into the 'analytics' category. These are differentiated from standard reporting tools in that they incorporate progress against business objectives into their answers. Problem areas or hotspots can be highlighted to executives by means of simple traffic light mechanisms so that executive time can be spent here and not on areas that are working effectively.

All of the software vendors we spoke to cited the growth of interest in Human Capital Asset reporting as a major driver behind their investment in these technologies. A common message was that senior executives are less interested in 'HR data' than in how it can be combined with other data assets in the organisation to answer directional questions for the business.

The purpose of such tools may be summarised as an attempt to standardise the non-standard. While managers may take pride in their organisational capabilities, at the most senior levels there is frequently a requirement to display powers of disorganisation; that is the ability to ask difficult and disruptive questions about the status quo. At this level the functional distinctions of HR, Finance and Customer data disappear; the job of HR Business Partners is to ensure that their data is closely aligned and integrated with other forms of data in the organisation.

THINGS TO REMEMBER

- Requirements for HR technology should be driven by a clear understanding of the service design and operating model for HR which, in turn, is driven by a common agreement on the service the business really needs.

- Be sure to engage with your IT team early on in the process, so they fully understand the objectives, drivers and outcomes of the transformation and can support them accordingly.

- It is critical to ensure you have fleshed out the requirements for the service before embarking on developing the IT requirements. This will ensure that the service drives the IT solution and not the other way around.

- Incorporate the likely MI requirements at all levels in the organisation.

③ Making the Case for Technology

INTRODUCTION

Building a robust business case to justify expenditure on new HR technology is often one of the most challenging parts of the overall process. HR organisations that have not thought through their business case thoroughly before taking it to the board for approval may find that not only is their case thrown out but that the very purpose of HR can be questioned along with it.

Lack of preparation at this crucial stage can spell disaster. For an organisation of any significant size or complexity, the costs of purchasing and implementing an HR information system can run to many hundreds of thousands, if not millions, of pounds and the HR practitioner must expect to face questions along the lines of:

- What will it enable us to do that we can't do now?

- Can't we do more with the systems we already have?

- Why does this cost so much – can it be done cheaper?

- Why do we need to spend money on this when we can get more value from spending it on customer service/our stores/front line services/developing our managers, and so on, and so on?

Thus the debate around the need for investment in HR systems is very closely aligned to the debate about whether HR is a back office support function whose overheads should be minimised or a force that can have a material impact on the commercial success of an organisation.

In the past, HR has often relied on fairly basic arguments to support the need for an HRIS, particularly at a time when the organisation had no automated HR systems. Arguments tended to focus on the ability to make operational improvements but often with rather imprecise savings implied, for example:

- 'Better absence information will bring down the absence levels in the organisation.'

- 'Integrated document production will reduce time spent by HR in the recruitment process.'

While these arguments may be true they lack credibility if they cannot be quantified and shown to have a direct influence on the ability to reduce costs or improve service in a measurable way.

Improved absence information will only bring down absenteeism as part of an absence control initiative and so the benefit of investment in HRIS is indirect. More importantly, reducing absenteeism will not automatically result in savings unless returning staff are productive when they return to work; implying a need for wider performance management systems rather than just absence management.

Similarly, arguments relating to savings in HR staff time are only really valuable if they result in genuine headcount savings or create the opportunity to do something that could not be done before. Saving an HR administrator 10 minutes a day does not, generally, provide a real benefit to the organisation. More importantly, such arguments rely on the viewpoint that 'HR is an overhead that must be reduced' and neglects to look at the ways in which HR's contribution to the business and, ultimately to shareholder value, may be enhanced by the introduction of new systems.

What is often missed is the potential that HR systems offer to bring about transformational change in the HR function enabling the introduction of new models of operation such as Shared Services and Business Partner teams. Such changes are instrumental in delivering significant operational savings and improving the quality of service that HR offers to the business. Thus the biggest benefit that HR systems can offer is the ability to support a reorganisation of HR services.

Within this chapter we will look at the process of building a comprehensive and coherent case for investment in HR technology based on a clear understanding of how the system will bring about improvements in the way HR services are delivered.

PREPARING THE BUSINESS CASE

The approach taken in preparing a business case may vary considerably between organisations, with significant differences in the required level of detail and the rigour with which the costs and benefits are assessed.

Some of the most rigorous demands for investment appraisal are found in public sector organisations with strong obligations to protect public funds from profligacy. The level of detail demanded to support public sector IT investment is often cited as a reason why projects in this sector can be so difficult to get under way and why the public sector often lags the private sector in technology development. However, it is interesting to note that public sector IT projects are among the most successful, with many being able to make a direct connection between the level of investment and the results seen in the organisation.

For organisations that view HR as an overhead, the arguments for technology tend to be focused on reducing that overhead – 'how can we reduce HR headcount or other operating costs?' But in organisations that value the strategic contribution of HR and seek to drive increased performance and competitive behaviour through the use of best practice people policies, the case for technology will be centred more on service enhancement and competitive advantage.

Generally, the business case will be used to drive a decision at senior levels on whether the proposed expenditure on HR transformation technology can be justified and whether the project can proceed. We have looked at the issues relating to the preparation of a robust business case against a number of headings:

- Using consultants to support the business case.

- Preparing the cost model.

- The benefits case.

- Selling the case to the board.

USING CONSULTANTS TO SUPPORT THE BUSINESS CASE

The initiation of the business case is often the first point at which the organisation may consider engaging with outside parties to support the project. Certainly there is no shortage of organisations willing to offer 'independent' and even 'free' advice on the process of establishing a business case.

The need to identify detailed cost estimates to support the business case will frequently involve obtaining quotes on software licenses, technology architecture and implementation services from established suppliers of HR software. Requirements for long term support for the HR system may require engagement with specialist IT outsourcers who can provide such services. Similarly, if the new service delivery model for HR is dependent upon elements of outsourcing (for example, for payroll processing or recruitment) then additional suppliers in these markets may be consulted.

Organisations of any significant size or global complexity may already use applications such as finance or procurement systems from the major ERP providers such as Oracle or SAP. As a consequence these suppliers may have dedicated account management teams operating at senior levels in the organisation whose specific job it is to understand the business context of new projects and, of course, position their own solutions. Many of the major suppliers routinely provide 'free' services to help the HR practitioner develop the business case for investing in new technology.

Given that suppliers are ultimately attempting to make a sale; how valuable are these services and how accurate is the business case information they provide? (see Table 3.1) Our own experience is that there are often some highly experienced individuals in these supplier organisations who have a good understanding of how technology can add value to the prospective client and they can have a lot to offer. However, there can be drawbacks to this approach that the possible buyer needs to take into account.

It is in respect of this last point that organisations may choose to work with major consulting firms to support the development of a transformation led business case. This is undoubtedly where much of the expertise is located but such firms often also maintain large systems implementation teams who rely on work from specific software suppliers. In short, major consultancies may take a broader transformational view of the business case but may have a bias in favour of a particular supplier that is not immediately apparent to the organisation using their services. Clearly, the claim to be an 'independent advisor' should be carefully examined.

It is important to recognise, too, that, as the requirement for HR information and process support is explored in more detail, the complexity of the proposed solution may increase. For example, opening up self-service applications to remote locations may create business requirements for new software, hardware and network infrastructure as well as hosting and support. Indeed, as the business case is developed, the

Table 3.1   Using   software   suppliers   to   support business case development

Advantages	Disadvantages
• Services are often provided at no charge. • Individuals may be highly knowledgeable about HR technology and provide valuable guidance to the process. • Suppliers may have an intimate knowledge of the organisation and its business needs through the activities of their account teams. • Suppliers should be best placed to advise integration issues around their products and the benefits arising from this. • Ability to reference to other organisations.	• Software suppliers have an agenda – their business case will almost inevitably support the purchase of their product. • Findings may not be transferable to other solutions hence options from other suppliers for delivering the organisation's requirements may not be considered. • In our experience, suppliers tend to focus on the ability to make incremental improvements in operational costs or service levels. Suppliers themselves are rarely equipped to advise organisations on how to implement transformational change in HR through the application of technology.

organisation may wish to explore the impact of many different scenarios on the business case, for example:

- Outsourcing some part of the process such as payroll.

- Using best-of-breed applications for specialist functions such as learning management.

- Considering the use of hosted IT services.

- Variations on the functional scope or geographic coverage of the system.

Once different options for delivery start to be factored into the business case, the dependency on external organisations to provide elements of the costs increases significantly and it is highly unlikely that a project team working solely with internal resources will be able to scope and cost a solution accurately enough for the business case.

Many HR programme managers will have led this process before and be quite comfortable with the prospect of managing multiple suppliers, each with their own agenda. However, for the uninitiated, the assistance of an experienced practitioner in this area can help to avoid some costly mistakes and focus the business case on truly important issues. Such advisors should demonstrate some basic characteristics.

For example, independent advisors should not receive payment from a supplier or be reliant upon that supplier for a major part of their business. They should also be able to provide clear guidance and opinions on the way forward. A consultant who will not come off the fence is of little use to the project team who will need clear answers as to the relative strengths and weaknesses of the solutions offered.

PREPARING THE COST MODEL

Failure to take a comprehensive view of project costs will result in weaknesses in the business case that may be pulled apart under scrutiny. However, pinning down the component parts of the costs of a solution can be complex and frustrating work. On the one hand, suppliers, while keen to push the advantages of their product, may be reluctant to present costs for a wide range of modules for fear of sinking the business case. On the other hand, an internal team may take the cautious view that the costs should be presented as a 'worst case scenario' and take account of all eventualities, thus making the project non-viable before it gets off the ground.

Clearly, a middle way is required that provides a thorough and honest appraisal of the solution costs while ensuring that the principal variables affecting costs have been pinned down as far as possible. Cost components that should be considered are outlined in Table 3.2.

Table 3.2   Cost components for the HRIS business case

Software Licenses	Providers typically sell licences to organisations to use the different modules of their software. Additional costs may be incurred for the use of the suppliers underlying database products and management information tools. 'Bundled' deals incorporating many different modules of a suppliers solution should be looked at closely to ensure proper fit with the scope of the project. Timing is also a factor as the project may not have need of some modules until later phases of the project which may be months, and even years away.
Cost per employee	An alternative to charging a licence fee is the move towards charging on a 'per-employee' basis, whereby the organisation is charged a specified rate per year for each employee. Such arrangements are increasingly common with suppliers offering 'software as a service' type solutions where the system resides wholly on the supplier's hardware and usage is effectively 'rented' to the organisation. Such arrangements can be highly attractive to organisations looking to smooth out the high initial costs of purchasing and implementing a new system.

Table 3.2   *Concluded*

Technical Architecture	The design and configuration of large scale networks and support infrastructure are specialised skills in their own right and care should be taken that the project engages the appropriate technical resources in order to avoid underestimating costs for inclusion in the business case.
Application Development and Delivery	This covers a wide range of activities associated with the delivery of the new solution. Development and delivery relates predominantly to the people costs associated with implementing systems and is particularly important if third party resources are to be used rather than internal. Key stages of the implementation process are discussed later in this book.

THE BENEFITS CASE

In some organisations the benefit case for investment in HR technology is taken as read, it simply being a case of defining how the functions and information provided by the new system will work in support of the accepted HR strategy.

For other organisations it can be an uphill struggle, often related to the historical perception of HR as a mainly administrative function that adds little value to the organisation. However, making the case for investment is not as difficult as might first appear if it is tied effectively to other planned changes in the HR organisation; moving from a traditional to shared service model is of course the most striking example.

HR system benefits usually fall into the following three categories:

1. *Hard, or direct, savings* are defined as strictly tangible cash savings arising directly from the introduction of new technology. Tangible costs are defined as those that reside in a clearly identifiable cost centre that may be reduced by a specified amount in coming years. Specific types of hard benefit include:

   - *Headcount savings* – Headcount savings can be taken when staff numbers are reduced as a direct result of implementing the new system. Typically, this arises from savings based on isolated improvements in operational efficiency or, on a larger scale, through a reorganisation of the way in which HR services are delivered. More significant savings are achievable through, for example, reorganisation of HR transactional activity into a SSC offering the opportunity to re-engineer 'end to end' processes. The introduction of self-service tools to allow line managers and staff to manage their own data and processes also provides the opportunity to remove HR intervention (and headcount) from the process. It is not unusual for savings of 25 to 30 per cent of operational HR headcount to be achieved if transformation is successfully delivered.

   - *Technology savings* – The decommissioning of old systems in HR is likely to generate some level of cost saving in its own right. An important consideration in the replacement of legacy systems is the current cost of ownership, where the cost of support and maintenance can be very high. Outgoings associated with the current system may include software licence maintenance and support; internal and contracted IT support costs and hardware/server maintenance.

2. *Soft, or opportunity, benefits*: Opportunity benefits arise, as the name suggests, because the new system presents an opportunity to realise savings that were not possible before. Critically, opportunity savings do not accrue directly from the system but require further management action for which the outcome may not be fully certain. Examples of opportunity benefits include:

- *Reducing absenteeism* – The provision of effective absence data may allow the organisation to undertake new absence management initiatives. While estimates may be made of the impact of such a reduction they are also dependent, in part, on the effectiveness of management action and therefore cannot be credited to the HR system alone. Similar arguments may be deployed around opportunities to reduce staff turnover.

- *Reduction in third party costs* – The use of third party suppliers to support critical or high volume activities such as recruitment is a regular feature of many HR functions. Modern web-based recruitment functionality may provide an organisation with a unique opportunity to take a corporate view of recruitment and reduce reliance on external agencies. Again, similar arguments may be made around training, pensions and payroll where more sensitive operational HR data can be used to track the effectiveness of external suppliers in driving cost reduction and service improvement opportunities.

- *Avoidance of errors* – Data entry errors can clearly cause inconvenience or profound irritation but may also have a monetary impact. For example, research undertaken by ADP and YouGov highlighted that 20 per cent of employees will not report a payroll error in their favour. Clearly the ability to reduce errors in the payroll function will produce a measurable benefit.

- *Revenue generation* – Whilst HR itself may have limited opportunities to generate revenue it can have an impact on other roles that do. For example, faster recruitment and induction of sales and account management staff coupled with improved performance management and development processes may have a tangible impact on new sales revenue. Calculating the impact of such initiatives may be a delicate exercise that needs to be coordinated with the sales function.
- *Cost avoidance* – If it can be argued that 'Y' can be saved if 'X' is spent and this can be identified as a budgeted cost then this can be included in the business case. A typical example would be the avoidance of the need to upgrade the old HR system in the coming year by replacing it.

3. *Service level improvements* – A central part of any business case will be tying the technology investment to the positive impact on the quality of HR service delivery, which in turn may be linked to what other changes to the service are delivered in parallel with the new system. Particular areas where a case for improved service can be made include:

- Improved data integrity and accuracy.
- Faster response to queries.
- More accurate, better informed decisions.
- Faster response to requests for MI.
- More effective trend analysis and the potential to initiate proactive management.
- Improved service levels to external candidates.

–   Better focused and targeted training initiatives.
–   Reducing risk by eliminating service failures and missed data entry through error.
–   Alignment of HR to the business agenda, providing the opportunity to create a dedicated resource for generalist advice/centralisation of operational tasks.

The above list is not an exhaustive representation of the benefits that an HR system can deliver and much will depend on the level of rigour the organisation wishes to apply to the investment process. Some types of benefit will typically find more favour than others; hard benefits by their nature provide a guarantee that a saving will be made and therefore are likely to be viewed in a more positive light. Unfortunately, the ability to save IT costs and make headcount savings may not be sufficient to justify the cost of new systems.

Greater benefits may be identified in areas of opportunity savings. The impact of reducing absenteeism, expressed as a percentage of payroll, may be huge. There is not always a clear guarantee that these savings can be achieved, however, so such benefits may be less well regarded in the business case.

Finally, the opportunity to improve HR service levels or drive a reorganisation of HR services may provide real long-term commercial advantage to the organisation but is hard to quantify. Our experience suggests that the most successful business cases paint an integrated picture of how each type of benefit may be realised from investment in new HR technology.

SELLING THE CASE TO THE BOARD

Getting sign off to the project may vary from a highly formal to a completely informal process. Typically any large-scale investment will be reviewed by the executive or an appointed board and will be subject to some form of financial appraisal. Although a robust business case is essential, it may be insufficient on its own for an executive that requires specific detail about how the benefits will be delivered.

In organisations that make specific use of the Prince2 methodology to deliver projects, the term Project Initiation Document (PID) is used to describe a document encompassing sufficient information to describe what will be delivered, how it will be done and who will do it. The PID would typically be presented to the executive at the same time as the business case and would work in support of it. The contents of a typical PID are described below in Table 3.3.

Table 3.3   Contents of a Project Initiation Document (PID)

Context	This provides background to the project – why it is needed, what it will cover (and not cover), what it will look like, and what are the main assumptions, risks and constraints. It may consist of the following headings: • Background. • Vision, Scope and Objectives. • Assumptions. • Risks. • Constraints.

Table 3.3   *Continued*

Project Approach	This section describes the approach which the project intends to apply to the remaining stages:

Selection – use of partners (for example, for implementation) and proposed selection process.

Design/Build – how will design be conducted (for example, use of requirements workshops, and checkpoint meetings for users to review the configuration).

Testing – for example, in a payroll project, how many parallel runs will be undertaken and will this be based on a sample of records or the whole population.

Training – outline training needs analysis and proposed approach, tools, location, resources and so on.

Business Change and Communications – assessment of the impact of the proposed changes and the readiness of the business to undertake them.

Implementation Phasing – for example, will all applications be launched as a 'big bang' or will roll-out be phased; will their be a pilot; will there be implementation waves or will the whole organisation go live simultaneously.

Data Conversion – what approach will be taken to converting the historical data which has been identified as needing to be transferred from the old to the new system? |

Table 3.3   *Continued*

	Data Capture Requirements – will any new data be needed, for example, position details if organisational management is being implemented for the first time; will any existing data need to be cleansed (for example, email addresses in an HR CRM project) and how will this be achieved? *Proposed Technical Approach* – how the different technical environments and resources will made available and deployed during the project; will some of the coding be outsourced? *Major Cutover Issues* – will any significant interim arrangements be needed immediately before, during or after launch?
Project Plan	Many projects fail because timescales are too optimistic. Starting with the major deliverables, stages and milestones the project plan should reflect the following: *Major Deliverables* – the key outputs from each stage, for example, user requirements document, system specification, system configuration and so on. *Key Stages and Milestones* – a high level plan showing the main stages (for example, feasibility, selection and delivery) with their start and end dates, and the major milestones which each stage will accomplish (for example, package chosen and purchased). *Tasks and Resources* – a more detailed breakdown of each stage showing the main tasks and who will do them, with resource estimates.

Table 3.3 *Concluded*

	Dependencies – key dependencies both within the project (for example, user acceptance testing cannot start until the system test has been signed off) and external to the project (for example, installing the servers depends upon the new data centre being built). *Critical Path* – linked tasks which cannot slip without delaying go-live. *Contingencies* – how the project plan could be flexed to cope with critical difficulties. *Quality* – showing the measures proposed to ensure that quality assurance is planned into each key stage and deliverable, and how will this be monitored.
Project Governance and Control	*Governance* – Project governance describes the means by which senior stakeholders in the client organisation, often in the form of a steering committee or project board, oversee the project and make critical decisions such as authorizing commencement of key stages and agreeing major changes. Project Board members should be fully empowered to make the necessary decisions on behalf of their functions or businesses and should meet as regularly as needed. *Controls* – various control mechanisms are available to project managers and should be used appropriately, even if a formal methodology is not being followed. These include risk, issue and change management, progress reporting mechanisms, and regular reviews of progress against plan and budget.

We now have a clear statement of the problem, the proposed solution, and how the project intends to deliver it together with a business case that describes the associated costs and benefits of the project. This represents all the information required to agree and sign off the overall business case. Depending on the level of investment involved, the business case may ultimately be signed off at board or executive committee level. The project manager is accountable for ensuring that the cost and benefit data is consolidated into a formal financial appraisal. Typically, where a large investment is required this will be scrutinised by the Finance Director, and must be robust.

The contents of a formal financial appraisal will vary between organisations but might typically include:

• Analysis of the completeness of costs.

• Validation/audit of proposed benefits.

• Calculation of organisation-specific measures of business case value (for example, internal rate of return, net present value of expenditure).

• Recommendation to proceed.

The complexity of some of these analyses leads many project managers to engage the assistance of a project accountant to ensure that the financial appraisal is properly completed. Although these constitute a substantial pack of documents, they are a sensible and necessary prerequisite to securing approval to proceed to the product selection and investment appraisal stage, with all the effort and involvement with third parties that this will require. Each document so far produced will be re-used, developed further or referred back to as the project proceeds, so none of the work will have been wasted.

Completing a robust business case provides a basis for logical decision making when it comes to investment. It is wise, however, to focus on engaging the key decision makers and their advisers throughout this phase of work. Significant time has very often to be invested by the project manager in enlisting the support of the various individuals who make up the board before the final decision to proceed. This may even be critical where there is a communication gap or poor relationship between some of the key players such as the Finance Director, the Chief Information Officer, and the HR Director. Thorough stakeholder engagement will help ensure there is sufficient senior sponsorship to secure the required investment and drive the project forward.

THINGS TO REMEMBER

- The most potent arguments in an HRIT business case lie in demonstrating the potential for HR systems to bring about transformation change in HR.

- External consultants may provide support in developing a complex business case but their credentials as 'independent' advisers should be carefully examined.

- Effective business cases rely on a combination of hard benefits, opportunity savings and service improvements to demonstrate a balance between realistic cash savings and the potential to drive longer-term commercial benefits.

- Project appraisal processes may typically require more than just a cost and benefits case. Detailed information on the planned project approach, activities and milestones and project governance may be required as part of a full project initiation document (PID).

(4) Selecting the Right Vendor

INTRODUCTION

Once the business case for investment is approved, then the project team is potentially let loose on the market with a large sum of money burning a hole in their collective pockets.

Perhaps the analogy with a shopping trip is not entirely fair. Many organisations will have carried out their vendor selection exercise in parallel with the development of the business case and may have a very clear idea of which products and services they wish to buy. Other organisations may have simply carried out some rough research for the purposes of the business case but left the selection process until final approval has been gained.

At whichever stage in the process you arrive at vendor selection, it is worth bearing in mind that this may be the first time the market is alerted to your intention to spend money on a new HRIS solution and this will inevitably bring you into contact with the sales organisations in different suppliers.

The sale of software and services is one of the biggest industries in the world, accounting for annual revenues in excess of

10 billion Euros in Europe alone. As might be expected, the sales professionals who work in this industry are highly skilled at pressing their agenda and influencing organisations in favour of their solutions. Organisations that enter the market looking for the right solution need to have developed a good understanding of their own needs so that they can assess the market effectively and objectively and make sure the process meets their agenda and not the supplier's.

Approaches to procurement vary enormously depending on the processes in place in each organisation. They may range from an afternoon spent at a software show picking up brochures to a full-blooded public sector procurement process lasting many months. In this section we will provide some pointers to the elements of a procurement process that make for successful buying decisions.

WHAT MARKET ARE YOU IN?

In Chapter 2 we considered how the organisation should go about defining its requirements for HR technology. So what does this tell you about which elements of the market might provide the right solution for your organisation?

Figure 4.1 provides an overview of the typical solutions on offer in the market for HR and payroll solutions. Although there are literally hundreds of systems available, the main differentiation is between what we have termed Tier 1 and Tier 2 solutions.

	Functionality	Flexibility	Integration	Cost
TIER 1 SUPPLIERS • *ERP solutions – integrated back office applications including HR, Finance, Procurement* • *Global delivery capability* • *Principal benefits arise from integration and the capacity to manage an end-to-end process across functions* • *Market dominated by SAP and Oracle*	Comparable - self service - workflow - web based - performance mgt - resourcing - L&D	Highly flexible – tailorable to a wide range of requirements. Level of integration demands consistent view of process	Key differentiator for Tier 1 – ability to integrate back office process across regions	Complex organisations demand costly solutions and delivery Battle for mid market – Tier 1 & 2 increasingly in each others traditional markets. Low cost Tier 1 options appearing
TIER 2 SUPPLIERS • *Niche players focused on HR/Payroll market* • *Different offerings from "best of breed" suppliers versus fully integrated solutions* • *Historic focus on SME market* • *Principal benefits are in cost and ease of deployment* • *Regional focus*	Good range of core functionality Best of breed suppliers offer more functional products in specific areas	Configurable to different requirements but with limitations on the functionality of configured elements	Focus on passing data via custom interfaces – can bottleneck processes	Rapid deployment – with minimal configuration

Figure 4.1   HR systems market overview

THE TIER 1 MARKET

The Tier 1 market is dominated by the giants of the industry, major Enterprise Resource Planning (ERP) system providers who provide HR applications as part of an integrated suite of business applications that also include Finance, CRM, Procurement and Manufacturing solutions. Such solutions tend to be large and complex and may be wholly unsuitable for many organisations. The principal benefits offered by ERP solutions relate to their global nature and ability to share data across geographically distributed organisations in different legal environments. They also enable the integration of HR data with other types of management information such as finance data.

Organisations that wish to consolidate HR management information across a world-wide operation to produce, for example, global compensation and succession planning data may look to a Tier 1 supplier to meet their needs. Similarly, organisations wishing to integrate HR and Finance data to produce accurate information for resource planning and costing may need the integration offered by an ERP solution. Bear in mind that a sophisticated requirement may not necessarily be related to a high number of employees. Many organisations employing only one or two thousand people will need to manage global HR processes and may therefore find themselves in need of Tier 1 functionality to support operations in multiple countries and produce global MI.

THE TIER 2 MARKET

We have termed suppliers that do not fall into the above definition 'Tier 2' although, as might be expected, this is not a definition they tend to use themselves. Key characteristics of Tier 2 solutions may vary but would typically include a focus on the SME market (small and medium enterprises) and possibly on one particular geography or related geographies (for example, focusing on the UK and regions with similar employment legislation such as Hong Kong). This might be of no consequence to organisations that are not widely dispersed but would be a major constraint for an organisation seeking a global HR solution including operations in the US.

Tier 2 suppliers might also tend to focus on products that cover one functional area or related areas. For example, many suppliers cover the HR and payroll markets; some may additionally cover related areas such as pensions administration or time management solutions but would tend not to provide solutions to support Finance or procurement.

This could be seen as a distinct benefit by organisations looking for the focus that an HR specialist may bring but it could also create overhead in terms of the cost of integrating HR and payroll systems from one supplier with solutions from different suppliers in other parts of the organisation.

As might be expected, the market is rarely as clear cut as is suggested above, and many HR specialist suppliers are now making inroads to the global market. The framework does still provide a useful reference point when considering where a particular set of solutions fits in.

WHO DO YOU NEED TO LOOK AT?

Having decided what type of solution you are in the market for, the next task is to determine whose specific products you wish to look at. For organisations working under strict public sector procurement rules this may not be an option. Many of them are obliged to invite expressions of interest from all suppliers in the market and will issue pre-qualification questionnaires for this purpose. This ensures that no suppliers are unfairly closed out of the process too early but it does add to the overall elapsed timescales of the process.

In different circumstances a more pragmatic approach may be preferable. For many, the logical starting point is to draw up a list of around half a dozen suppliers that may have the capacity to meet your requirements and from whom you would like to seek a formal response. In some cases this list may be self-defining.

For example, a large organisation, employing in excess of 30,000 employees globally and with complex geographical and integration issues, will only have a choice of the large ERP vendors of which two, SAP and Oracle (incorporating Oracle

PeopleSoft) dominate. Other factors such as a predetermined IT strategy may constrain the choice further; for example, if the organisation has elected to build all of its systems on the SAP platform.

For others the choice may be much more open. A useful place to start is many of the software exhibitions that are staged throughout the year, the CIPD and Softworld HR technology shows in Europe and the IHRIM conference in the US being good examples. Exhibition guides provide a large amount of comparative data on suppliers' products and complementary trade press articles are frequently published at around the same time.

Deciding who to shortlist may also be driven by other factors and stakeholders in the organisation. The IT function may have technical platform requirements which require solutions to be based on particular technologies. Some suppliers provide products specific to certain industries, such as construction, which are relevant to the organisation and which may already be in use. Although not necessarily yet at the formal tendering and evaluation stage, many organisations choose to review the market with a series of vendor visits and supplier demonstrations simply to enhance their view of what is already available on the market.

One issue to be aware of is the rapidity with which software solutions develop and change over time so information and opinions that are valid one year may not be the next. For this reason it is often valuable to seek opinions from expert advisors who maintain an up-to-date market knowledge of HR systems and can advise on the relative merits of each. Again caution should be applied to the selection of an advisor to ensure that their 'independent' credentials are robust. Independent advisors should receive no payment from software providers for recommending their products and, most importantly, should not be selling services that relate specifically to a particular supplier's products (for example, services to implement a specific solution). Orion Partners are always happy to provide a fully independent view of the current market for HR and payroll solutions.

WHAT DO YOU NEED TO BUY?

Having identified a list of likely candidate suppliers the next stage is to determine what they have to offer and to obtain formal proposals and price quotations. Our own research suggests that most organisations use less than 25 per cent of the HR system functionality they actually purchase which is a damning indictment of the way in which we source business solutions.

Much of the problem lies in the way in which software solutions are sold. Suppliers will routinely offer bundled deals for their software solutions where several modules are offered at an attractive discount price. Such deals can seem less attractive, however, when the organisation realises it will be required to pay maintenance on all the modules it purchases regardless of whether it implements and uses them.

Software is not the only commodity likely to be on offer; it is increasingly common for software vendors to 'partner' with the major consultancies offering implementation services as part of a 'total solution'. Project teams may find that their software selection process is inextricably linked to decisions on what external consultancy services to acquire also and it is equally important to understand what is being offered here.

So how can the organisation make sure that it acquires only what it intends to use? As part of the market review process you will likely have looked at several different suppliers of HR solutions and may have received demonstrations of their solutions. However, until you enter the selection stage you may not have received a formal proposal from the business describing the services and products they intend to supply. This is an essential step that ensures you have a clear view of how the suppliers' solutions will meet your requirement and precisely what the implications are in terms of costs, effort and resource required to implement them.

The most comprehensive source of information on what is needed lies in the requirements document. A key part of any selection process involves mapping your requirements to the solutions that are on offer to gauge the level of fit and to establish what the final costs will be.

The vehicle for a formal approach to a supplier may take many forms but is often referred to as an Invitation to Tender (ITT) or Request for Proposal (RFP). The purpose of an ITT is to provide suppliers with the information they require to make a sales proposal to you. Information contained within an RFP may vary but will typically include:

- Information on the organisation and the current business context.

- Background to the project and the business drivers for change.

- Comprehensive description of the functional and technical requirements of the new system prioritised according to business benefit.

- Questions for suppliers relating to their credentials, past experience, approach to implementation and reference sites.

The RFP is typically issued to suppliers with the expectation that they will provide a written response to the questions. Suppliers would be expected to confirm that their product was able to meet the requirements set out in the document and, if included in the scope of the RFP, confirm how they would approach implementation. The RFP would also require suppliers to provide a detailed breakdown of costs set out in a standard format so that the offerings of different suppliers can be compared side by side.

An overview of the typical contents of an RFP document is set out in Figure 4.2.

WHICH ONE IS BEST?

The process of seeking an RFP from a supplier should provide a comprehensive view of the solution and the services on offer but will typically result in the return of a large amount of information. Suppliers responses to questions on how they will meet your requirements, how they will approach implementation, what their experience is and who their current customers are, responses can typically run to several hundred pages. Multiply this by a shortlist of 6 or more suppliers and there is a lot of data to sift through.

Software evaluation typically involves the efforts of several different stakeholders including HR and payroll representatives at senior and junior levels, business representatives, IT, Finance and Procurement. One way of making the process

HR RFP : Table of Contents

1   **Introduction** ....
    1.1 Background...4
    1.2 Objectives...5
    1.3 Principles of operation 5
    1.3 Scope and phasing of the project 6
    1.4 Instructions to Suppliers 8
    1.4.1 Bid Logistics...
    1.4.2 Timetable for Response ....
    1.4.3 Submission of Response..
    1.4.4 Additional Information ....

2   **Commercial considerations**..
    2.1 Conditions...9
    2.2 Specification 9
    2.3 Cost Model..10
    2.3.1 Software Licence ....
    2.3.3 Hardware ....
    2.3.4 Ongoing maintenance ....
    2.3.2 Implementation delivery...
    2.4 Warranty 11
    2.5 Confidentiality 11

3   **The Requirements**...
    3.1 Functional Requirements..12
    3.1.1 Functional Priorities ....
    3.1.2 Supplier Scoring ....
    3.1.3 Detailed HR Functional Requirements ....
        3.1.3.1 Recruitment and Resourcing Process...
        3.1.3.3 People In Process ....
        3.1.3.4 Changes Process ....
        3.1.3.5 Absence Process ....
        3.1.3.6 Reward Process ....
        3.1.3.9.1   Payroll Inputs..
        3.1.3.9.2   Payroll Processing...
        3.1.3.9.3   Payroll Outputs and Interfaces..
        3.1.3.10 Grievance and Disciplinary Process ....
        3.1.3.11 Learning & Development Process – Performance Management.....................
        3.1.3.12 Learning & Development Process – Other...
        3.1.3.13 People Out Process ....
        3.1.3.14.1 Organisational Management ....
        3.1.3.14.2 Strategic Planning ....
        3.1.3.15 Reporting requirements...
        3.1.3.16 Workflow; Manager and Employee Self-service – ....
        3.1.3.17 Data Integrity and Security ....
        3.1.3.18 Interface Requirements -...
        3.1.3.19 Technical Architecture –..
        3.1.3.20 Volumes ....

4   **Delivery** ....
    4.1 Delivery Partner Strategy 56
    4.2 Implementation Partner Profile 56
    4.2.1 Experience and Expertise...
    4.2.2 Resources..
    4.3 Implementation Approach..57
    4.4 Project Plan 57
    4.5 User Training Requirements 57

Figure 4.2   HR RFP table of contents

more manageable is to give different members of the team responsibility for evaluating different areas of the response.

Given the volume of information provided it is also advisable to develop some form of evaluation plan to keep track of suppliers responses in different areas and to allow the evaluation team to 'score' and compare suppliers' responses. Typical areas covered by a formal evaluation plan are illustrated in in Table 4.1.

Table 4.1 **Typical areas covered in a formal evaluation plan**

Evaluation area	Key questions
Functional Fit	• How closely does the product meet the requirements set out in the requirements specification? • Will the solution require customisation to meet requirements or are they met as standard? • Are there any functional areas where the product is weaker than others?

Technical fit	• How well can the supplier meet the expressed IT requirements for:
	  – Integration.
	  – Scalability.
	  – Back up and recovery.
	  – Data integrity.
	  – Security.

Implementation approach	• How well defined is the implementation approach, milestone plan and deliverables? • Will the system be implemented by the supplier or an accredited implementation partner? • Does the implementation approach provide for adequate project management, change management and quality management? • How experienced are the proposed team?

Table 4.1 *Concluded*

Evaluation area	Key questions
Vendor	• How credible is the vendor in terms of their experience in the HR market, in the geographies covered by the organisation and in the relevant industry sectors? • Do they have a sound customer base and track record in delivering the product they are proposing? • Are they commercially robust and financially sound? • Can they provide a relevant reference site?
Business understanding	• Do they show an awareness of the commercial issues faced by our organisation? • Have they tackled similar issues elsewhere? How did they address them? • Have they understood our requirements and do they have sensible proposals as to how they will be met? • What other value added services can they provide us with?
Compliance and bid logistics	• Have they maintained a good, professional attitude towards us as potential customers throughout the process? • Have they adhered to deadlines surrounding the bid process? • Are their responses complete and consistent?

The above questions represent only a proportion of the total set of criteria by which a supplier might be evaluated. The number of criteria will depend on the depth to which you wish to go in any particular area and the level of interest from different members of the team. One approach is to set up a formal evaluation scoresheet (Figure 4.3) that compares responses in different areas and allows team members to score responses. An element of weighting may be added to differentiate areas that are proportionately more important to the business.

Vendor 1	Score 1-10	Score 1-10	Total Score	Potential Maximum Score	% Score
Credibility and track record in HR and Payroll	6	8	48	60	80%
Understanding of Industry	4	5	20	40	50%
Customer base and track record in the UK	8	5	40	80	50%
Reference site relevence	5	0	0	50	0%
Reference site response and review	8	0	0	80	0%
Long term robustness of company	6	7	42	60	70%
TOTAL	37		150	370	41%

Figure 4.3   Example vendor scoresheet

Some elements of the scoring may be completed after the receipt of the initial proposals from suppliers resulting in an initial evaluation and, quite possibly, a reduction in the long list of suppliers (see Figure 4.4). The next stage of the process is typically to seek detailed demonstrations from suppliers to obtain further information and to answer any remaining questions in the plan. Once the process is complete, the evaluation plan should provide an audit trail of the decision making process and allow anyone outside the process to understand how the selection decision was reached.

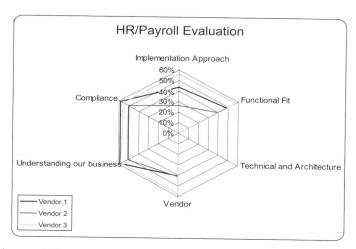

Figure 4.4   Summary vendor scoring

WHAT DOES IT DO? – SURVIVING THE SOFTWARE DEMONSTRATION

As discussed above, once the initial evaluation of the RFP is complete the organisation will likely wish to make a series of supplier visits and see software demonstrations with the shortlisted suppliers. On one level, the software demonstration is merely an extension of the evaluation process that started with the RFP. However, this is often the first opportunity that many in the team will have had to view the products they have been considering and, for some, this may be their first sight of a modern HR system and what it can do. The principles of dividing up responsibility for evaluation areas among the team and continuing to use the evaluation plan and scoring mechanisms to keep track of how requirements are met remain important.

Suppliers are usually very happy to have an opportunity to host prospective customers and show them the capabilities of their products. Most suppliers are very good at this process and will have staff whose sole job it is to demonstrate the product to new prospects; a role that combines in equal measure a knowledge of HR process, of the system and its capabilities and a flair for showmanship!

Whilst it is reasonable to expect that a supplier will want to show their solution to its best advantage they should not be allowed to dominate the proceedings with flashy but irrelevant demonstrations of functions that are not required. Likewise, long, lovingly photographed videos on company history or the Chairman's charitable works do not have a place in the demonstration room where the evaluation team has assembled with a specific purpose, and time is precious. The following list (Table 4.2) sets out some of Orion Partners' best practice tips for getting the most from software demonstrations.

Table 4.2   **Orion   Partners   top   tips   for   vendor demonstrations**

1.	***Prepare the day well***: Assembling a large number of people in a room to evaluate a software solution does not make for a naturally orderly process. Ensure you have discussed the agenda in advance with both the evaluation team and the software supplier so everyone knows what you want to achieve. If possible set expected timings for each area you want to cover and make sure that you do not overrun at the expense of other critical areas.
2.	***Beware of opening demonstrations***: Whilst it may have occupied large parts of your thinking for several months, demonstrations of software can be a little dull. To counteract this, suppliers often start with a demonstration of some of the more sexy aspects of their solution, often relating to the production of advanced management information and workforce metrics. Whilst such demonstrations can be useful in the right circumstances, they are not particularly helpful if you have come to look at a payroll solution. It is a good thing if the supplier is creative in their demonstration but try to make sure they keep it relevant.
3.	***Be clear what solution is being demonstrated***: Software solutions develop at a rapid pace with vendors updating their products often on an annual cycle. In addition, suppliers may periodically bring out completely new products designed from scratch to take advantage of changes in the technology market. Be clear on what product is being demonstrated and if client organisations and numbers of users are quoted make sure these relate to the product you are buying.
4.	***Stick to your agenda***: Make sure the day is kept relevant to you and keeps to the agenda items you have requested. Make sure that all the areas you want to evaluate are fully covered.

Table 4.2 *Continued*

5.	***Be prepare to shake up proceedings***: Don't be afraid to stop the demonstration and refocus the remaining time if you are not covering ground quickly enough or if you have got away from the critical areas. Taking an evaluation team out for a day to a software supplier is a big investment in time and it is imperative to get the most from it. Most software suppliers will be quite willing to reorganise the day to suit you as they will be fully aware that you need to make an informed decision.
6.	***Divide and conquer***: Not many HR specialists want to sit through a detailed payroll demo and comprehensive discussions on database security will only interest a limited number of the team. If you have several areas to review and evaluate, be prepared to divide the team up and arrange separate demos of different areas.
7.	***Be clear on the implementation approach***: If your vendor visit also covers the topic of implementation, make sure that sufficient time is allowed to discuss this. If possible ask to be introduced to the person who would be your project manager to test your reactions to them. Check the level of resources available in the team and the number of live projects they have running; do the numbers add up or will your project be in danger of being under resourced? Get the project manager to talk through the plan and highlight any areas of concern they might have, do they sound credible and experienced? Lastly, make sure you are clear on the level of input that is required of you and the split of responsibilities between you and the vendor's team. If you wish the vendor to take more responsibility than they have planned for, what will this do to the costs.
8.	***Be insistent***: Do not allow your questions to go unanswered. Credible suppliers will have no difficulty in answering your concerns and will generally be patient to ensure you have what you need. Be very wary of a salesperson that gives an indirect or woolly answer to your question.
9.	***Go to them***: If given the choice always elect to visit the supplier on their own premises.

Table 4.2 *Concluded*

10.	***Take references***: Following up with reference site visits is another key part of the evaluation process. Reference sites are generally customers, like you, who have already bought and implemented the solution and can provide you with a view on the capabilities of the system and their experience of implementing it. Suppliers should be prepared to allow you to speak to reference sites alone but will probably wish to set up the call or visit out of courtesy to their client.

FINALISING THE SELECTION DECISION

The stages above describe the broad elements that might go into a selection decision although, as discussed, the actual path taken through the process may vary considerably. Public sector organisations, bound by procurement rules, may add stages to the process to gain a broad view of available products in the market before issuing a full invitation to tender. More flexible organisations may choose to forgo some of the formality of a tender process by settling on only one or two suppliers with whom to carry out an accelerated decision process.

While it is important to make an informed decision there may be merit in considering an accelerated approach to selection, particularly if other factors constrain the choice of systems. For example, many large or complex organisations may decide early on that their choice lies between the two ERP giants Oracle and SAP and a detailed evaluation process may show some critical differences between the two solutions. However there is also an argument that says the difference between the market leading solutions is marginal and effort spent on selection would be better spent on aspects of the project that have a greater impact on project success such as the choice of project manager. Thus an accelerated approach to selection may pay dividends in terms of time and attention to other aspects of the project.

At the end of the demonstration stage, the evaluation team would typically be close to a position where they can make a decision. Additional information may be sought from the supplier as an adjunct to their demonstration, reference sites may be followed up and a final review of the scoring process should indicate where the overall preference lies.

At this stage it may be necessary to update related documents such as the project plan and approach and the detailed cost elements of the business case.

THINGS TO REMEMBER

- There is no fixed process for selecting a software solution; be prepared to vary the approach taken according to the needs of the business and the demands of the procurement process.

- The market for HR systems may be differentiated by organisational size, geography, IT integration or functional requirements. Ensure you know which apply to your organisation and which products are most relevant.

- Utilise external consultants to help research the market only if they offer a truly independent service.

- Use the mechanisms of the RFP to engage with suppliers and make a formal assessment of the products and services you truly need.

- Make decisions based on a common understanding of what each solution offers.

- Test each supplier against a common set of criteria that assess their ability to ensure your project is successful.

⑤ Designing and Implementing the Service

DESIGN AND IMPLEMENTATION

As we have seen in Chapter 1, the successful delivery of HR transformation is critically dependent on the supporting technology infrastructure. This section considers the principles that should be applied to the delivery of an HR technology architecture and its main components.

Delivery of an HR and Payroll system and related technologies is a major undertaking in any organisation and the process of system delivery requires careful planning and management to ensure a low risk approach and a successful outcome. A comprehensive description of the process of system delivery could fill this book many times over and will not be attempted here. Instead we have confined this chapter to presenting an overview of the main stages and what they comprise so that their purpose may be better understood.

Delivery projects of this nature are usually managed in four broad phases as illustrated in Figure 5.1.

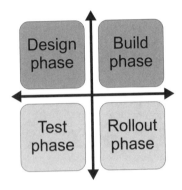

Figure 5.1   HRIS project phases

The whole process is managed under tight day-to-day project controls by the project management role which we will describe first before going on to cover the phases shown above.

PROJECT MANAGEMENT AND CONTROL

Project management is a set of principles, practices and techniques applied to the leadership of project teams and to the control of project schedule, costs, quality and risks. Complex projects require excellent management and the role of project manager is critical to the successful delivery of HR technology. However effective the project's methodology, technology or team, it is unlikely to succeed without a capable project manager.

The project manager's prime objective is to deliver the project within *timescale* and *budget*, and to the required *quality*. Achieving success against these parameters in the case of a large and complex HR transformation technology project involves a wide range of skills, knowledge and experience on the part of the project manager, including:

- Authority, credibility and presence.

- The ability to lead, motivate and develop the project team.

- Drive and 'stickability'.

- A results orientation.

- Exceptional communication and influencing skills.

- A high level of judgment and political 'nous'.

- The ability to move seamlessly between macro and micro-management.

- Experience of managing projects of similar type, scale and complexity.

Project managers have at their disposal a number of mechanisms for controlling project delivery. These should be used appropriately, to achieve effective project management without enmeshing the project team in layers of bureaucracy that place form-filling above delivery. Some of the more commonly used techniques and principles are described in Table 5.1.

A key aspect of project management is the ability to engage and work with third party suppliers. Organisations increasingly rely on 'rainbow contracts' to deliver complex programmes; contracts that allow them to engage a range of suppliers with core skills relating to each of the different delivery areas.

When you engage with your IT supplier, whether your in-house technology team, the software supplier, or a consulting

Table 5.1   Key components of project management

Key components of Project management	Key principles and techniques
Risk management	Logging key risks, including an assessment of their potential impact and probability of materialising or controllability. The routine logging of risks provides a basis for planning to reduce risk elements and to ensure adequate contingency plans are in place.
Issue management	Log issues as they arise, assess them for their impact and develop mitigating actions. Ensure issues are closed out speedily.
Progress reporting	Regular reporting is needed at programme, project and workstream level, to ensure a balanced view of progress is maintained and communicated, and that major issues are visible and can be addressed. Progress reporting may be managed through the production of weekly workstream reports, and assessments of the status of each workstream as Red (off track), Amber (off track but with plans in place), Green (on track).
Plan monitoring	Project plans may be maintained within packages such as MS Project and enable each task to be recorded, along with 'baselined' start and end dates, associated resource, and dependencies. Tasks are typically grouped according to key project 'milestones' and the data presented as a Gantt chart illustrating critical path activities.
Benefits tracking and budget monitoring	The business case spreadsheet should be updated regularly with actual figures and revised forecasts in the form of monthly costs and benefits, and changes in anticipated spend and savings.

Table 5.1 *Concluded*

Key components of Project management	Key principles and techniques
Quality control	Performance against the quality plan should also be monitored, to ensure that delivery is to the required standard. Quality criteria should be associated with key deliverables, and it is important to ensure that time is built in for quality reviews, with results logged. Some project methods may require completion of gate criteria to assess whether to proceed to the next stage.
Change control	As the project proceeds, it is likely that new requirements will emerge or that issues will force a different approach to delivery, for example, it may prove necessary to customise the package (see below) because its functionality proves to be insufficient. Change control requires that all impacts of proposed changes to scope or approach are assessed in terms of cost, timing and impacts across the project.

services firm, it is critical that the solution developed fits your requirements and is delivered to required timescales. This list of hints and tips highlights things you should consider in building this relationship:

- *Don't sign any contracts until you are happy with them.* Although there is always significant pressure to start the project, it is imperative you understand and are content with what is contained within the contract for any third party delivery. The supplier will be heavily invested in ensuring your project is a success, but ultimately the contract is your primary tool in obtaining value for money for your organisation.

- *Insist on meeting with, and vetting, the key IT team roles.* It is imperative you and the wider team have a good working relationship with the IT project or workstream manager, and the Business Analysts responsible for the design. Typically you would expect them to have prior experience of the application, of delivering solutions for HR and, ideally, of working in the relevant industry sector.

- *Take time to present the project context, aims and objectives to the IT team.* In particular, focus on the overall service design principles for the final service. The more the team understand what you are trying to achieve, the more likely they are to be able to help you.

- *Ensure you understand your suppliers and how they work.* In particular, their drivers and priorities. For example, an in-house IT team may find it difficult to incorporate additional work without deprioritising another project. Make sure you understand and are comfortable with the contingency that has been allowed for unplanned or uncosted activity at the start of the project.

- *Ensure you are clear about the split of responsibilities within the IT team.* It is easy to assume that because you have engaged with a number of different IT leads you have covered all bases. Are you clear on who is responsible for data migration? Who will be conducting performance testing to ensure the solution can cope with the required volumes of users? Ideally all technology related activities will be driven through your IT project or workstream manager but this may not always be the case.

- *Don't be driven by the IT methodology.* Many organisations have IT methodologies they use in the delivery of systems, together with a set of standard document templates they use to define the key deliverables. You and your team of HR and business experts will be accountable for the sign off of many of these documents, in particular during the design phase. Have the IT manager take you through the key steps within the methodology, the templates used and completed examples. Don't be afraid of requesting modifications to the process or templates to improve useability from the wider project team perspective.

- *Discuss and agree the quality control criteria you will use as part of the document acceptance process.* This will mitigate any design issues that arise as a result of the misinterpretation of poorly worded or ambiguous documentation. This is key where development activity is offshored as the build team will develop exactly what is described in the design documentation. Where there is ambiguity, they may be tempted to fill in the gaps with an inappropriate solution in order to meet build timescales, rather than coming back to the team to clarify specific points.

- *Make sure you have sight of the detailed IT plans,* and you understand the dependencies and risks associated with the work scoped. Ensure IT representation is included in the project or programme governance and clear channels of communication are established. Regular communication will minimise the likelihood of any nasty surprises cropping up during the build and test phases.

- *Don't be afraid to ask for more information.* Supplier teams often tend to work in isolation to the rest of the project, in particular during the build phase. Ensure you have early sight of work in progress, for example early demonstrations of functionality, to make sure the solution is progressing in the right direction. Prompt the team for early training of your UAT team during the planning phase, and for relevant documentation that will help inform the UAT test criteria.

- *Ensure the supplier team are involved in the planning and needs analysis for the training solution.* Where there is a significant component of IT change, part of the training solution will focus on actual use of the system, within the wider context of the processes and roles that underpin the transformation. Many applications include specific tools that can be used to deliver IT specific training, while classroom based training still represents a viable alternative for many organisations. The involvement of the IT team will be imperative, in particular from a planning perspective where training development can overlap with the busiest period for IT, resulting in a resource constraint.

THE DESIGN PHASE

The design of the chosen solution involves the development of detailed documentation defining the structures, roles and processes needed to deliver the new service. As part of this process, specifications are also defined that will determine how IT systems are configured for use by HR and the business.

Because most organisations will be using package based technology, the emphasis will be on determining how the package can best be configured, using the tools provided, to meet the specific needs of the organisation. This is analogous to adjusting the controls on a TV set to obtain the perfect picture; it is quick to do and does not affect the underlying operation of the TV.

Staying within the limits of a system's configurability will avoid the need for customisation. This is where a requirement is so complex or so far outside the standard functionality that to meet it changes would be required to the source code that underpins the system. Customisation of a package is undesirable for a number of reasons:

- It demands a rigorous approach to programming the system adding significant levels of cost and risk to the project.

- The customisations will not be supported by the supplier.

- The customisations may cease to work when the supplier releases periodic upgrades to their software.

Many project failures can be traced back to an early decision to develop some bespoke software in pursuit of a particular requirement.

Therefore, the design process, if run well, will both question any requirements that look as though they require customisation of the solution and endeavour to find ways in which they can be configured as part of the standard application.

The key element of challenge required to deliver an effective design is in questioning whether a potential requirement for customisation is critical to the effective running of the business, or whether a modification to the process is acceptable. It is important to maintain objectivity in these discussions as both end users of the system and the guardians of IT design may have a vested interest in the outcome of the decision. Early development of design principles that are observed throughout the design phase is an excellent way of driving the design work to a useable and maintainable solution.

The design requirements are usually elicited through a series of workshops, involving several parties:

- Users who can articulate the requirements in business terms.

- Business analysts who can lead the workshops and translate the user requirements into system language.

- Configurers who are skilled in the use of the chosen package and will go on to build the system.

It is absolutely vital that all key stakeholders are represented at the workshops and that they have empowered their representatives to make decisions during the sessions. If this does not happen, the process will falter because key design decisions cannot be reached or because key stakeholders subsequently contradict design decisions.

In the case of a package approach, solution design should reflect the package modules and it is usually sensible for the workshop programme to reflect this structure. In an HR system project for example, workstreams are likely to be required for resourcing, learning and development, payroll, time and attendance, employee administration, reward, employee relations, organisation management, management information, interfaces, security and access and data conversion.

In addition to the process of running design workshops other project tasks that need to be considered now include the following:

- *Testing strategy:* which defines the overall approach to testing the completed solution and processes.

- *Training strategy:* including a training needs analysis and examination of the types of training to be used.

- *Business change and communications strategy:* incorporating an assessment of change impact and business readiness as well as the planned strategy for communicating the planned change to stakeholders.

- *Implementation planning:* including planned approach, phasing, activities and dependencies.

- *Support approach:* defining how end users will be supported during and subsequent to go-live.

- *Technical model:* The technical model developed during the initiation/feasibility stage should be refined to reflect the chosen package and design.

- After the workshops are complete, the design specification documentation (often termed the 'blueprint') should be finalised and issued to key stakeholders for sign off. This document is critical to the process that follows and serves two main purposes.

- It describes the solution in enough detail to allow business users to confirm that it describes the solution they require.

- It is sufficiently detailed to allow the configurers to build the solution.

A good strategy to ensure swift sign off is to empower workshop attendees to recommend the blueprint to the stakeholder for their area for sign off. This ensures that it is the business rather than project team members who present the solution for confirmation.

BUILDING THE SOLUTION

The build phase should largely focus on configuring the package according to the specifications identified in the design phase although this stage is also where interfaces to other systems are developed. Key stages of build activity and related activities that need to be considered at the same time are described in Table 5.2.

Table 5.2   Solution build activities

Solution build	Activities
Package configuration	Involves configuration using the tools supplied by the solution provider. This stage of the process may provide for interim reviews of the solution by users to determine whether the solution being built matches what they have signed off.
Development	This covers any inevitable non-standard build elements (that is, additional to configuration) for example interfaces, data conversion programs, enhancements, non-standard reports or forms. The configuration team will typically translate the functional specifications into technical specifications as the basis for developing computer programs. Well written technical specifications are critical to avoid costly and time consuming errors and re-work.

Table 5.2   *Continued*

Solution build	Activities
Data collection	If a significant quantity of data has to be gathered manually, planning for this should be underway. Examples include: • Organisation data, in the case of a new HR system which involves holding organisation data, relating to jobs and positions in the organisation, for the first time. • Email addresses, for example where self service is being introduced that will generate email requests and reminders to staff and managers relating to self service transactions. • Absence management: If there has been no single system for recording absence through sickness and holiday it may be necessary to collect data such as leave entitlements and leave taken to date before the system can become operational.
Data cleansing	HR data should be maintained accurately as a matter of principle and law, so all organisations should have ongoing procedures in place to achieve this. From a project standpoint, certain types of data (such as salaries and grades) have to be 'valid' for the new solution to be able to process it. If these have not been recorded in a consistent format in the past then this data will need to be reviewed and confirmed for all employees in the organisation.
Documentation	During the build phase, detailed work procedures will typically be prepared to document business processes and related usage of the system. The documentation would typically include detailed process descriptions and screen shots and will also inform subsequent stages of activity such as test scripts and training content.

Table 5.2   *Concluded*

Solution build	Activities
Test preparation	Immediately after the build stage is complete then the process of system testing will begin. Therefore, at this point a number of activities will be underway in preparation for the testing phase including the development of detailed test plans and specifications, set up of the technical infrastructure to support training and identification of resources for the testing workstream.
Training preparation	Also during the build phase, detailed preparation for training will typically get underway including sign off of the training needs analysis, preparation of course materials and set up of training facilities.

COMMUNICATIONS AND BUSINESS CHANGE

Customers should by now have been given initial notification of any major changes to the service arising from the project, and any initial briefings for local management should have been held.

It is important to maintain a continuous process of reaffirming the primary purpose of the HRIS change and the value it will deliver.

Our experience suggests that change is most effective when all parts of the business, from the top down, engage fully with the proposed process and technological change. Some common success factors for managing change include:

- Assign clear roles to key stakeholders in the communication process. Ensuring managers, in particular, are properly briefed and can identify and address employee concerns.

In this process, the change team need to coordinate the messages of executives and managers to ensure the consistency and accuracy of the message.

- Train line managers in communicating change. Managers will benefit in this process from an understanding of basic communication techniques as well as preparing them to deal with resistance to change and employee reactions to change. It is also useful to provide communication guides that address key talking points, FAQ's and anticipated employee concerns.

- Clarify communication channels and sources: Give clear direction to stakeholders about who to contact with questions and feedback regarding the new HRIS so they, in turn, can direct staff questions appropriately.

- Clearly communicate what behaviour needs to start, stop and continue in the new model.

TEST PHASE

Three types of testing are predominantly relevant for HRIS projects:

1. System testing – whereby the various teams involved in the development of the system ensure that the components of the system work individually and in an integrated manner.

2. User acceptance testing (UAT) – whereby users of the solution ensure that it successfully supports the end-to-end business processes.

3. Parallel running – In the case of a payroll project, UAT should include one or more parallel runs alongside the old system to ensure that the same results are produced.

A fourth area relating to technical testing would typically cover performance testing, security, backing up and restoring processes and so on. We have not considered this area of testing in detail.

SYSTEM TESTING

The system test involves testing the solution by running test scenarios using pre-written test scripts, the results of which can be compared with pre-defined 'expected' outcomes. The test should be based on design documents, for example, process maps, data definitions, functional specifications and detailed work procedures. Its purpose is to identify where the system accurately reflects the design and to confirm it is working correctly, so that errors or 'bugs' can be corrected and re-tested before it is released for user acceptance testing. As such, it is a fairly mechanistic process which is normally carried out by the solution delivery side of the project team – either by the suppliers/implementation partners themselves, or by a testing team resourced from within the client IT organisation. The UAT plan should include a schedule indicating which tests are to be performed on which days and by whom. The testers will then work through the scripts, logging the precise details of any fault or issue.

USER ACCEPTANCE TESTING (UAT)

The purpose of the UAT is to test the relevant business processes from end to end to ensure the solution operates satisfactorily and supports the original business requirement. UAT should ideally be carried out by the business people who agreed the design and who will become the actual users of the solution.

As with the system test, a detailed UAT plan should be prepared and worked through with faults being logged for resolution and re-retesting. At the end of the UAT, a report is prepared, describing performance against plan and acceptance criteria, and summarising any outstanding problems.

PAYROLL PARALLEL RUNS

In a project including payroll, a key aspect of testing is the parallel run, the scope of which may be defined as:

- Testing that the gross to net (GTN) programme within the new system generates the same calculated results (gross pay, net pay, deductions, employer's NI/pension contributions and so on) as those generated by the old system.

- Testing that payroll outputs and reports, for example, BACS payments, payslips and postings to other ERP solutions.

Parallel run testing is an additional safeguard carried out on payroll systems because of the high impact of going live with a system that does not function correctly. Parallel testing is intended to provide increasing levels of confidence to payroll management and users that the new system will achieve the above aims.

Several other types of test may be performed in the course of a comprehensive test programme.

TECHNICAL TESTING

A summary of the main test types, including those already referenced, is set out in Table 5.3:

Table 5.3   Types of testing

Test	Purpose
System testing	A broad term encompassing a range of tests carried out by system developers to ensure the components of the system perform in line with the technical specifications and that they operate in an integrated manner with each other.
User acceptance testing	Whereby end users of the solution ensure that it successfully supports the end to end business processes.
Parallel running	Where the system involved is a critical application (such as a payroll) running the new system in parallel with the old to ensure both produce the same results.
Performance and volume testing	Ensures that the hardware is capable of supporting the required numbers of users, transactions and data volumes, at peak as well as normal loadings.
Destruction testing	Attempting to 'crash' the system, for example, by hitting irrelevant keys.
Technical feature testing	Testing elements of the hardware and software infrastructure, for example, how the system copes with hardware or database failure partway through a transaction.
Regression testing	To demonstrate that the introduction of the new system will not adversely affect other live systems. This is particularly important in an ERP solution where the HR/payroll or CRM solution may share a platform with other modules, for example, finance which are already live.

ROLL-OUT PHASE

A critical decision within larger organisations is the order in which the new solution will be rolled out (see Table 5.4). Discussions regarding this will usually take place during the design phase and, in particular, once the impact on the business case and the associated system are fully understood. Discussions should be finalised in advance of the roll out phase. Options include 'big bang' (that is, going live with all functionality across all geographies simultaneously) and phasing by geography (adopting a phased approach by process or business unit). Typically implementations are usually 'big bang' or phased by geography as these options minimise the need for complex interim arrangements where temporary processes are needed to enable end-to-end processes to run.

Once the system tests have been signed off the system is almost ready to be rolled out to the organisation. Training courses in the use of the new system can now be delivered. These will typically use specially created training data running on a special area of the new system.

Like UAT, the training is ideally process based and will include system and non-system components. This ensures that agents and other users are trained in the end-to-end business processes together with responsibilities, accountabilities and overall objectives, not just in the use of the technology. Trainees may be assessed at the end of each module and will complete training course evaluation sheets so that the effectiveness of the training can be monitored. After training they may be given access to a 'sandpit' version of the system where they can gain further familiarisation with the systems at their own pace before being given access to the final solution in the 'live' or 'production' environment.

Table 5.4   Rollout preparation activities

Preparation for rollout	Activities
Support	Check that plans and service level agreements are in place with the supplier and in-house IT to define the post go-live support arrangements, for example, help desk, supplier telephone support and so on.
Business change and implementation	The project should by now be approaching the final and most intense phase of the business change process. Briefings and communications with the main customer representatives in the business should have taken place at regular intervals in the run up to go-live.
Live environment ready	Ensure the final version of the systems is loaded onto the 'production' environment by the IT specialists, so that it is ready for live use.
Local PCs	Local PCs and printers should be readied for live operation, with user access and passwords in place.
Data capture	Check that all data capture, for example, email addresses is complete, with any necessary interim procedures in place to keep them up to date ahead of go-live.
Interfaces	Check the schedules for interfaces from the new system and ensure any initial interface runs to update peripheral systems such as telephone directories are scheduled to run immediately prior to cutover.
Rehearsals	One or more dry runs of the cutover process will demonstrate that it can be accomplished safely and in a timely manner.

CUTOVER

When final preparations are complete, the Project Manager should provide a report to the Project Board on training delivery and cutover preparation. This report should list the previously defined go/no go criteria for the cutover decision, together with an assessment of the degree to which each has been satisfied, to give an at-a-glance view of readiness for go-live.

Once the Project Board has confirmed the decision to go-live the actual cutover tasks are likely to include the following:

- Conversion programmes are run against appropriate live systems so that they are populated with data. When the data has been converted it will need to be reconciled to ensure that it has migrated across correctly.

- Additional data that cannot be converted may need to be entered manually on the live system before normal operation can commence.

- User access profiles are unlocked so that users can access their systems.

- The project teams and key users are available on stand-by to deal with any last minute issues.

- The HR function gets to work and the users start to use the new system.

PROJECT CLOSURE

Once the project is live, the following checklist (Table 5.5) of items should be reviewed:

With these tasks accomplished, the project is complete and the new system is now under operational control.

Table 5.5   Closure checklist

Closure checklist	Activities
Review outstanding issues	A list of all outstanding actions and issues should be prepared recommending how they should be addressed.
Check availability of system documentation	All system documentation should be confirmed as having been completed and available to relevant support teams and users.
Archive non-operational documentation	All project/programme documentation which is not relevant to supporting the live operation should be confirmed as having been completed, and then archived.
Review project performance	A post-implementation review should be carried out to: • Assess overall project performance against the business case. • Highlight lessons learned. • List outstanding tasks showing how and by whom they will be actioned.

THINGS TO REMEMBER

- The skill and capability of the project manager is often the most critical factor in determining project success or failure; ensure that adequately qualified personnel are resourced to run the project.

- Configure, don't customise! Use the capabilities and embedded processes of the supplied package as far as possible. Adapt business processes rather than changing the source code of the system; it's easier, cheaper and less risky!

- Run design workshops with the right people in the room. Ensure the team running the workshops challenge assumptions and 'old ways of working'.

- Don't underestimate the importance or complexity of the testing process. Make sure that every aspect of the system and the associated business processes are tested.

- Ensure the business is adequately prepared for the business change and that people know what impact the system will have on current ways of working.

- Maintain a close track on all associated workstreams including areas such as data capture, data cleansing and cutover planning. Whilst these may seem remote from the heart of HR activity they are nonetheless critical to system success.

- Carry out a post implementation review and ensure lessons learned are carried forward into future project phases.

- Finally, implementation of HR and payroll systems is a complex task that requires specialist support. This section has provided an outline only of the key tasks and responsibilities at each stage. Inexperienced practitioners should seek specialist input to the planning and project management process and refer to more comprehensive texts on the subject. We recommend *HR Transformation Technology* – by Allan Boroughs, Les Palmer and Ian Hunter. Gower 2008.

⑥ Top 10 Tips for Success

So what are the principal lessons that the HR practitioner can take from the experts in delivering HR applications? In this final section we will explore some of the lessons from the collective experience of the HR managers, programme managers and end users who were interviewed as part of the background to this book.

1) SERVICE LED DESIGN

The impetus for many HR technology projects is to support delivery of the Ulrich model within HR operations. The main driver for such a change is the delivery of improved services and additional value at a lower cost to the business. However the disproportionate cost of the technology component can mean that the business becomes focused on a 'technically led solution' where solution delivery eclipses the true business motives of the programme.

A critical objective at the outset of an HR transformation technology project is the need to establish how the solution will integrate with the overall design of the HR function and, hence, to ensure an appropriate level of business focus on the technical project. The HR technology solution will need to be clear from the start how it will serve the needs of the SSC, the HRBP, the CoE, the line and the employees in the organisation.

The service ethos should be reflected in the service architecture for HR (particularly in the design of the MI strategy), the channel strategy for the service centre and the approach to knowledge management. Above all, technology is a tool for delivering business change – not an end in itself.

2) FOCUS ON THE BUSINESS CASE

The historical development of HR systems reflects the HR objectives that were prevalent at the time and does not necessarily reflect the requirements for delivery of service through the new model for HR. For most organisations, legacy solutions will not drive an HR transformation agenda because of their lack of functionality and of integration with the customers' needs, other back office applications and the business as a whole.

At the same time, the benefits offered by the transformation are defined in terms of service improvement and cost reduction and should be clearly articulated in the business case. If organisations fail to do this they will struggle to get past the large IT investment required to support the transition.

In the long term, a lack of investment in technology will result in systems that actually hold back organisational development. For many organisations this can develop into such a problem that it becomes significantly more attractive to consider the radical option of outsourcing HR process, together with supporting systems, to replace the capital investment required for the development of systems internally.

For the HR transformation programme manager, the need to demonstrate the value of HR technology and its direct linkage with the objectives of the change is critical. In short, the programme manager must quickly develop a grasp of the business case for investment in new systems and present this as part of the early planning for new solutions.

3) USE TECHNOLOGY INTELLIGENTLY

In any major HR change project, it is not unlikely that technology expenditure may account for 70–80 per cent of the overall budget for change. With such disproportionate spend it is easy for a transformation project to become technically focused and defined by technology deliverables and milestones such as testing, data conversion and technical integration rather than the delivery of benefits.

Our research shows that most large-scale ERP implementations deploy less than 25 per cent of the technology's available functionality. If nothing else, this would appear to support the suggestion that there is a divergence between what most technology projects can deliver and the reality of how the service will be used.

The onus is on programme managers to ensure that the programme maintains a proper perspective on the role of technology and the business objectives it is serving. It is their job to ensure that the business requirement is fully articulated (as opposed to merely written down) and understood before attempting to apply technical solutions.

Technology design and roll out should always make reference to the fundamentals of the project charter, specifically:

- How does this contribute to the business case?

- How does it improve service levels in HR?

- How does it reduce costs?

4) PARTICIPATE IN THE DESIGN PROCESS!

This may sound an obvious point but it is surprising how many projects delegate the design and development process to a third party, citing the need to 'rely on the experts' to guide them in the design of systems. While external expertise has a role in a systems delivery project, that is no excuse for abdicating accountability for critical design decisions affecting the way in which the application is used.

Any design process should place key users and stakeholders at the heart of the process. This can be achieved through carefully managed design workshops that deal with each process in HR in a detailed walkthrough with direct reference to the system. It is critical that users and stakeholders understand what they will be getting and the implications for HR process; it is not sufficient to obtain a user's signature on the bottom of a densely worded design document as evidence of 'sign off'.

The best designers will be able to articulate the planned design clearly and in a way that 'brings the system to life' for those who may be unfamiliar with what it can do. Detailed demonstrations, structured walkthroughs, proof of concept models and rigorous cross-examination of the design team are an essential part of the process.

5) INTEGRATION IS KING!

Once upon a time, HR systems were the preserve of the HR function with interfaces to other systems defined by the boundaries of the HR organisation. The new HR model extends demands for people data outside the boundaries of the HR function and creates the need for integration of HR data and process on a wide variety of levels:

- Within critical integrated functions in HR such as performance management, reward and development.

- Between the contact centre and the functional HR experts in Shared Services.

- For producing cross-functional management information spanning HR, Finance, Production and Procurement data.

While the main suppliers in the HR technology market have played out a 'functional arms race' to develop progressively more sophisticated applications, insufficient attention has been paid to the need for the integration of critical data across applications. For the practitioner selecting HR applications, attention to integration issues will pay far greater dividends than selection of solutions with a high level of advanced functionality.

6) PROJECT TEAM CAPABILITY, NOT SOFTWARE SELECTION, HAS THE BIGGEST IMPACT ON SUCCESS

Selecting the right solution is important to the success of the project but it is not the most critical factor. Many software providers can point to organisations that have implemented first class applications in an incompetent manner and failed to achieve any real benefit. Similarly there are many examples of low cost solutions that have been implemented intelligently and which deliver real strategic value to the organisation. The difference is, in most cases, the capability of the delivery team and, in particular, the programme manager.

Many organisations, however, focus intensively on software selection and neglect to spend anything like the same effort selecting someone with the appropriate skills to lead the project; in some instances even allocating this role solely on the basis of availability to do the job. Quite aside from the fact that the best person for the job is probably, by definition, the least available, this approach discounts the need for assessing critical skills and strategies to ensure the delivery is low cost, low risk and robustly managed.

7) MANAGE THE TRANSITION NOT JUST THE TECHNOLOGY

Separating the delivery of the technology from the drivers for the transformation is a recipe for disaster. It is critical that the focus of programme management is on the whole delivery programme. Successful transformation programmes are characterised by a number of key criteria:

- Early engagement with stakeholders to design a service that the business actually needs rather than one that is defined by the parameters of the technology solution.

- Development of an integrated '1 HR' model that ensures the primary relationships within HR work are fully integrated in terms of common process, knowledge sharing, service identity and shared values and purpose.

- Expecting and acknowledging that resistance to the change is likely. Tackle business resistance by building on early commitments, focusing on the basics that will make a visible early impact, and managing expectations.

- Establishing post-implementation disciplines in HR to ensure a commercial approach to service management, customer focus, monitoring and management of service performance and financial accounting.

8) PRACTICE GOOD PROJECT DISCIPLINES AND GOVERNANCE

Project management and delivery is a major topic in its own right and the secret of successful HR technology is, to a large extent, synonymous with good project disciplines. While these are too numerous to list here, key issues for the HR programme manager to consider include:

- Ensuring the critical project roles are in place including appropriate project governance and direction, senior level sponsorship and clearly defined project team roles and structures.

- Making intelligent use of project methodologies to ensure project delivery is properly structured without a slavish adherence to checklists and paperwork.

- Ensuring critical project deliverables are clearly set out and communicated; key documentation includes a current state assessment, clearly defined scope and vision for the project, the business case for change, the project initiation document and the operational model for HR.

9) CONFIGURATION NOT CUSTOMISATION!

Most, if not all, of the HR transformation technology solution will be based on package technology from mainstream solution suppliers. Programme managers should understand that the true value of package technology comes from the embedded business processes they contain. This represents the collective experience of the programme developers as well as all existing users who have contributed their experience to the overall design of the solution.

Against this background it makes absolute sense that the supplied process is the starting point for any design decisions. Customising the standard application is to be discouraged due to the risk, cost and support problems it creates and the organisation is well advised to change the process in preference to changing the system. More importantly, if the organisation discovers that it cannot deliver a 'standard' HR process using supplied functionality from a mainstream supplier then it may be a good indication that this process needs to be rethought.

10) ACT AS AN INTELLIGENT CUSTOMER

In many organisations an HR transformation technology project represents a major investment. It can be a massive undertaking involving large numbers of internal resources and the deployment of external expertise around key technical and change related roles.

It is easy to become overwhelmed in the face of so many expensively-suited consultants and defer to the greater knowledge that they bring. But it is a fatal error to place too much faith in the capabilities of your external advisers. In developing the solution, they cannot be expected to know as much about your organisation as you do. It is also in the nature of the consulting business that consultants will seldom admit publicly to being out of their depth and certainly not to the client!

At the same time, there is a wealth of previous experience available from external sources and the programme manager should seize the opportunity to learn from what others have done, understand how they benchmark against other organisations and seek expert opinions as to 'what will work here'.

The key here is to act as an 'intelligent customer', developing an active relationship with advisers that has several key characteristics:

- Asking intelligent, searching questions of your advisers to ensure due diligence. Seeking the views of consultants on the relevant issues and how they apply here, asking where they have encountered similar situations before and assessing their capability to tackle issues that present themselves.

- Insisting on good programme governance with effective project controls to identify problems early in the process.

- Taking an honest and direct approach to confronting performance issues on the team, wherever they lie.

- Understanding that no-one understands your organisation better than your own people and keeping control of key decisions around design and delivery.

- At the same time, understanding the value of partnership and how to make it work effectively. Success achieved by the consultant team will reflect well on them, the project and ultimately, you. Beating up on your consultants for every mistake or shifting blame for problems does not reflect well on anyone. Programme managers should develop an instinct for the things that are truly important to insist on.

SUMMARY

The development of HR systems has unrolled over the last three decades with much of that time spent establishing the functionality of the systems and the technical integration required to make them work effectively in an HR environment. There is now a wealth of options available to the HR practitioner to support the agenda for change in HR. Whilst the issues in delivering such solutions are complex, the rewards are high in terms of the potential for significant improvements in service levels and significant reductions in operating costs.

At the same time the fundamental shift in the organisation and delivery of HR services, initiated by David Ulrich and others, means that technology change now routinely happens in the context of a wider transformational agenda, aimed at delivering a more effective, value added HR service to the business. The success of such transformations rests on ensuring there is a clear understanding of where and how technology can enable the change, and equally importantly, where it cannot. The challenges in delivering such change are significant, and require a breadth of skills and capabilities from both the programme manager and the project team responsible for implementing the transformation. But the challenges do not end here. The ongoing opportunities associated with outsourcing, offshoring to new locations, managing technology upgrades, identifying and using new technologies and optimising assets all present the next wave of activity for HR teams.

In the course of this book we have tried to provide a guide for practitioners that steers a course through the complexities of systems delivery to achieve real and lasting benefits from technology solutions. We have reviewed the issues and decisions that must be taken from initial requirements development through to go-live and beyond. We hope we have been successful and that this book will become a valuable reference for your HR transformation journey.

Orion Partners

Orion Partners are leading independent advisers in HR Transformation. Established in 2002, we have led and managed HR Transformation programmes for over 30 blue chip clients and our client base covers leading organisations in both private and public sectors.

We help organisations to succeed in their HR transformation by enabling them to:

- Clarify and define HR's strategy and role relative to the business.

- Decide on the most suitable operating model for HR, including the option of shared services or outsourcing.

- Select and implement the right technology solutions.

- Assess and select the right people.

- Develop the skills and mindset to succeed.

- Make the transformation happen on the ground.

Our unique focus is the whole range of HR transformation activities. We pride ourselves on the independence and practical nature of our advice and our focus on identifying and capturing the benefits in our design and implementation. We have skills and expertise in scoping, design and change management of the transition.

We have a have a broad base of functional, industry and global experience. Together with deep knowledge of HR and what makes it work successfully. We undertake regular research in the HR field including our unique studies on the difference that makes a difference in HR Business partners and HR Leaders.

If you would like to find out more, please visit www.orion-partners.com or call us on +44 (0) 207 993 4699.

GOWER HR TRANSFORMATION SERIES

This series of short books explores the key issues and challenges facing business leaders and HR professionals running their people management processes better. With these challenges comes the requirement of the HR function to transform, but the key question is to what and how?

The purpose of this series is to provide a blend of conceptual frameworks and practical advice based on real-life case studies. The authors have extensive experience in all elements of HR Transformation (having between them held roles as HR Directors and Senior Business Managers across a range of blue chip industries and been senior advisors in consultancies) and have consistently come up against the challenges of what is the ideal new HR model, what is the value of HR, what is the role of the HRBP and how can they be developed?

Whilst the guides all contain a mix of theories and conceptual models these are principally used to provide the books with solid frameworks. The books are pragmatic, hands-on guides that will assist readers in identifying what the business is required to do at each stage of the transformation process and what the likely options are that should be considered. The style is entertaining and real and will assist readers to think through both the role of the business and transformation project team members.

SERIES EDITOR

Ian Hunter is a founding partner of Orion Partners, a consultancy specialising in providing independent advice to organisations considering outsourcing their Human Resources department. He has worked for a number of leading management consultancies, including Accenture and AT Kearney and has been an HR Director in two blue chip organisations.

If you have found this book useful you may be interested in other titles from Gower

Developing HR Talent:
Building Skills and Beliefs for the New HR Function
Ian Hunter, Jane Saunders, Allan Boroughs, Simon Constance,
Tracey Bendrien and Nicola Swan
Paperback: 978-0-566-08829-2
e-book: 978-0-7546-8167-0

Going Global:
Managing the HR Function Across Countries and Cultures
Cat Rickard, Jodi Baker and Yonca Tiknaz Crew
Paperback: 978-0-566-08823-0
e-book: 978-0-7546-8134-2

Managing HR Transformation:
Realising the New HR Function
Ian Hunter, Jane Saunders, Allan Boroughs, Simon Constance,
Tracey Bendrien and Nicola Swan
Paperback: 978-0-566-08828-5
e-book: 978-0-7546-8166-3

Visit **www.gowerpublishing.com/hrtransformation** and

- search the entire catalogue of Gower books in print
- order titles online at 10% discount
- take advantage of special offers
- sign up for our monthly e-mail update service
- download free sample chapters from all recent titles
- download or order our catalogue